SWV

STRATEGIC
WARFARE
VICTORY

Dr. Karen Deadwyler

Copyright © February 2013 by Dr. Karen Deadwyler

Published by
Dr. Karen Deadwyler
North Massapequa, N.Y. 11758

http://glorytempleministriesinc.ning.com

http://drkarendeadwyler.com

Cover designed by Shameka Montgomery of We Shine Design

All rights reserved. No part of this publication may be reproduced, stored in a retrieval system or transmitted, in any form, or by any means, electronic, mechanical, recorded, photocopied, or otherwise, without the prior written permission of both the copyright owner and the above publisher of this book, except by a reviewer who may quote brief passages in a review.

The scanning, uploading, and distribution of this book via the Internet or via any other means without the permission of the publisher is illegal and punishable by law. Please purchase only authorized electronic editions and do not participate in or encourage electronic piracy of copyrightable materials. Your support of the author's rights is appreciated.

All Bible verses are from the Holy Bible KJV.

Printed in United States of America

ISBN 978-0-9802390-6-5

Contents

Dedications 5

The Apostle 7

The Prophet 9

The Evangelist 10

The Pastor & Teacher 11

Warfare Prayer 12

Acknowledgments 13

Preface from the Lord 14

Prophetic Insight 16

Introduction 17

Chapter 1: Strategic 18

Chapter 2: Warfare 46

Chapter 3: Victory 72

About The Author 101

Bibliography 103

My mom Evangelist Pastor Pauline Owens

Dedications

"I will praise thee, O Lord, with my whole heart; I will shew forth all thy marvellous works."

Psalm 9:1 (KJV)

This book is dedicated to my mom *Evangelist Pastor Pauline Owens*. For truly we have learned a lot about *strategic warfare* together through our sickness, suffering and pain. The sickness, suffering and pain was only for a season but our spiritual growth that was excelled through it is for a lifetime. Nevertheless, To God be the Glory we made it through and now we live to declare the Glory of God and to tear down the kingdom of Satan.

What a *marvelous thing* God has done!!!

"This was the Lord's doing, and it is marvellous in our eyes?"

Mark 12:11 (KJV)

TO THE FIVE MOST IMPORTANT PEOPLE IN MY LIFE

To The One and Only True and Living God; this book is written out of obedience to the Lord. I will always praise the Lord for being my Savior, my Healer, my Redeemer, my Helper, my Counselor and most of all the Great I Am. The God that I serve is awesome in power, commands and in statues. Who would not want to serve a God like this?

To Ronnie Deadwyler my best friend and husband of twenty-five years and counting; look where God has brought us from. Like the Psalmist sings He has brought us a mighty long way in the natural and in the spirit. I still say Love Conquers All….words will never express my love for you. May God continue to bless this marriage and shine His light on you.

To my father and mother Pastor Clarence Owens and Evangelist Pauline Owens I love you because you are the greatest parents a child could ever ask for. Thanks for all your teachings and love and support. I could have never come this far without you two. May the Blessings of God overtake you!

To my sister Prophetic-Evangelist Denise Owens you will always be my big sister in whom I love and look up to. I love you for just being you and your uniqueness is a blessing to our family and to the Body of Christ. You have such great love and concern for people and your helping hand will always be blessed by God.

To all my family and friends that I cannot name one by one… Thank you for everything and all of your love and support during my lifetime. I love you all.

~FOREWORD~

~The Apostle~

As the modern day Church is preparing for the second coming of Jesus the Christ, demonic activity has reached an all-time plateau. The world is yearning for the manifestation of the Sons of God. One may ask, how are the "Sons of God" manifested in the earth? My resounding answer is "One must embrace and comprehend Strategic Apostolic & Prophetic Tools and Teaching" such as this Powerful and Anointed book.

I believe that God selects His choice Messengers to Apostolically and Prophetically teach the Body of Christ how to recognize when there is diabolical/demonic activity at work and how to defeat the enemy of the cross, which is Satan! The scriptures are full of strategies within its pages and God's chosen Messengers can rightly divide the Word of God; and has the ability to receive revelation from God to "pull out" the hidden nuggets to assist all believers to be victorious.

Apostle Karen Deadwyler is such a one. She has been chosen by God to write and reveal the tactics of the enemy. She has a divine understanding of Spiritual Warfare and how it can affect the move of God in the earth and in the life of the believer.

We are aware the world is without true knowledge concerning the human conditions. Some use natural plans, schemes and legislation to try and fix a spiritual battle. This book will equip the believer on how to overcome this world by utilizing Godly principles through strategic warfare. This tool is inspired by the Spirit of the living God for end time Victories!

All Christians will experience warfare and will need Divine tools to effectively fight our already defeated foe and emerge victoriously. It is imperative that all Believers regardless of one's title or position in the church should embrace Apostolic teaching regarding this topic. This book will open the understanding of all that will embrace this knowledge. This is a must read for today's Church!!-

I applaud Apostle Karen Deadwyler for accurately articulating the concepts of Spiritual warfare!

>   Apostle/Prophet DeShawne Coles
>   Destiny International Ministries Worship
>   Center Headquarters
>   ODC Ministries
>   Pittsburgh, Pennsylvania

~FOREWORD~

The Prophet

I am honored to write in support of this timely book written by Apostle Dr. Karen Deadwyler. She has the spiritual insight and leadership to write and share kingdom principles that can equip believers on how to strategically conduct spiritual warfare with the understanding of the things that God has given us. Therefore, this book is an empowerment tool of understanding so that believers do not fall into the traps of Satan.

Our fight is not with people but it is against the spirits of darkness in this world. I do believe that this book with assist you with composing and constructing strategic warfare so that the victory is manifested over the evil spirits that were created to kill, steal and destroy.

We are waging war over the spiritual kingdom of darkness and not people, therefore, launch true spiritual warfare and show no mercy and take no hostages.

>Prophetess Lougenia "Trailblazer" Rucker
>Divine Diamonds Ministries
>Philadelphia, Pennsylvania

FOREWORD

The Evangelist

The Devil (Lucifer) the fallen angel whom was cast down from the heavens has but one everlasting agenda for mankind which is to kill, steal, and destroy. It is with great honor and humbleness from God that I was blessed to be the sister of Apostle Karen Deadwyler, a true righteous servant of our Lord and Savior. There is not a better teacher that can arm you with the correct and most up to date information for going into warfare with the devil and come out winning and saving souls.

This is her true calling a position given to her by God which she rightfully accepted and has done a stupendous job with. As her sister I am overjoyed and rightfully proud that she accepted her position with no questions asked. But God the Father has a special crown awaiting in the heavens for the dynamic job she is doing and will continue to do.

In her newest compilation of writing Strategic Warfare Victory she has the mind of the reader engulfed in God's plan for their lives and leaves you informed on how to take back what the devil has stole from your life. To God be the Glory for helping her open up the heavens and revealing to her readers how the devil works in their lives.

Prophetic-Evangelist Denise Owens
Glory Temple Ministries
North Massapequa, New York

FOREWORD

The Pastor & Teacher

Dr. Karen Deadwyler's motto is "God what's Next? God in His vast Glory, power and wisdom opened the heavens and made a direct download of the Apostolic Anointing so that no man shall get His Glory. This book was divinely written prophetically and apostolically anointed to set the captives free and empower them to understand and operate in the word of God and in God's Ministry.

To God be all the Gory for all He has done and is doing. This is a masterpiece in the works! Chapter one "Strategic" is action packed, powerful, informative, eye opening and left me wanting to know more. It is so real that it challenges you to seek God for the truth. It is an in your face book, that unveils the real truth about life, its downfalls and how the world was created. This book speaks of the truth and nothing but the truth!!!!

It is a must read. It will bless you naturally and spiritually.

Apostle Ronnie Deadwyler, Sr. Pastor
Glory Temple Ministries
North Massapequa, New York

~Warfare Prayer~

Father in Jesus name as I write this book that you have ordained, Let your people know that there is victory in spiritual warfare through Christ.

May this book increase their wisdom, knowledge and understanding of who you are in the spirit realm.

May your people have a clear and concise revelation that Jesus has truly defeated and overcame all of the works of Satan; and through Faith in His name and the power of His Blood we can overcome too!!!

Amen, Amen, Amen
Dr. Karen Deadwyler
Copyright 2013

~ Acknowledgments~

I thank God for the Holy Spirit which gives me the knowledge, wisdom and strength that I need to write this book and to complete this assignment that has been bestowed upon my life.

I want to thank all my spiritual parents, mentors and everyone that has helped me become the women of God that I am. I could not have done it without your contributions to my spiritual walk.

To my church Glory Temple Ministries thank you for all the love and support that you have given me through the years. You are not only a church but a true family that has been there during our good times as well as through our struggles. I love each and every one of you and thanks for always pushing me and encouraging me to go forward.

To every student of God's Training Camp for the Fivefold Ministry thank you for trusting me to teach you in this new season. Many of the things that God had me teach as well as write in this book was from life's experience. You all encouraged me to hang in there and not to faint…

To everyone that supports Dr. Karen Deadwyler International Ministry's thank you for allowing the God in me to encourage, heal, bless and empower you through the Gospel of Jesus Christ.

To all the readers of my first two books "His Miraculous Way" and "Five Rights Medication for Your Soul" thank you for buying, supporting and promoting these books. Without readers we as authors would have no purpose to write; so thanks for empowering my purpose as a New Testament Apostolic-Prophetic Scribe…

~Preface from the Lord~

When I Dr. Karen Deadwyler sought the Lord for my next book to write; the Lord said "Write to my people about true spiritual warfare.

What is True Spiritual Warfare? Let's define each word according to a dictionary.

- **True-** real; genuine; authentic, not deceitful, being or reflecting the essential or genuine character of something.
- **Spiritual-** of or pertaining to the spirit or soul, as distinguished from the physical nature: supernatural.
- **Warfare-** armed conflict between two massed enemies, armies, or the like.

So as I define these words and put it all together and added the revelation of the Holy Spirit to it, my conclusion of true spiritual warfare is this: It is a genuine authentic supernatural spiritual battle (meaning it has nothing to do with what we see in the physical). It is a battle between Satan and God for your soul and spirit and whichever one wins the battle; that will be the results manifested in our flesh, physical existence, and in eternity.

Our physical manifestations can usually give us some indication of which way we are leaning towards. My question to you is: Is it God or Satan? Although we may know the answer sometimes we just need to be enlightened as to what is really going on around us.

True spiritual warfare happens daily and it is underestimated by the world and the Body of Christ. The Body of Christ needs to understand that true spiritual warfare is strategic (important in or essential to strategy).

So I present to you my third book; "Strategic Warfare Victory."

THE PROPHETIC INSIGHT

"Lest Satan should get an advantage of us: for we are not ignorant of his devices."

2 Corinthians 2:11 (KJV)

This book Strategic Warfare Victory will be the catalyst for change to many that will come in contact with it. "It will give you strategic guidelines from a Biblical perspective and teach you how to set yourself free from the enemies' schematics and devices that come against you daily"; saith the Lord.

Introduction

"The thief cometh not, but for to steal, and to kill, and to destroy: I am come that they might have life, and that they might have it more abundantly."

John 10:10 (King James Version)

I believe this is the best scripture to describe what I am trying to impart into your soul and spirit when you read and apply the principles from this book. This verse shows you that there are two outcome results from the realm of the spirit. One is Satan's desires for you (he desires to kill, steal and destroy you) and the greater one is God's desire for you (that you may have an abundant life overflowing with blessings).

God allows us to know that in this life there are two opposing forces going on in the realm of the spirit; one is of evil (that is Satan's Kingdom) and another one that is of good (this is God's Kingdom). The goal of this book is to teach you how to discern which spirits are operating in and around you and how to strategically beat the devil at his own game; better known as **strategic warfare victory**.

I

Strategic

"In the beginning was the Word, and the Word was with God, and the Word was God. The same was in the beginning with God. All things were made by him; and without him was not any thing made that was made. In him was life; and the life was the light of men. And the light shineth in darkness; and the darkness comprehended it not."

John 1:1-5 King James Version (KJV)

In the beginning was the Word, for many of us that means the Bible. On the other hand for those of us who have a deeper revelation of the written word (The Logos) we also know that scripture is talking about Jesus. According to New Testament scripture; Jesus is the Living Word. Now before we can talk about being strategic there must be some facts stated about what happened in the beginning. I mean in the beginning of the world, the beginning of mankind and the beginning of your own personal life. Surely you must understand that this book is based on the Bible and on this road we call life. When we look at the Bible we understand that everything pertaining to life must be referenced back to God.

So let's look at this scripture above and let us see if we can give you some unveiling and understanding of what it says. "In the beginning (before anything existed) was the Word (Jesus), and the Word was with God (The Bible), and the Word was God (the Trinity). The same was in the beginning with God (pre-existence). Then the scripture goes on to say all things were made by Him, which means everything that exists in this world God is the creator of it. Let me make it as clear as I can when it comes to the making of anything it is "all inclusive" from A to Z God created it. Nothing was made or existed before Him or was created by any other God but Him.

As we continue on in this scripture we read "In him was life; and the life was the light of men." In Him was life meaning God had the power and authority to create a living soul and that the life he created would be a light for all men to follow. This life and light (Jesus) that was created by God would become the light of the world and Satan which is the darkness in this world would never be able to understand Him or His ways. I said all of that to get to this point that in this world there are two distinct paths, there is a life full of light that's God's desire for you and a life that can be full of darkness and that is Satan's wish for you. In this road called "life" which path you take will be truly up to you. Nevertheless, my goal in this book is to awaken and enlighten you so that you will choose the right path for your life and that is the way of the light.

> *"Thomas saith unto him, Lord, we know not whither thou goest; and how can we know the way? Jesus saith unto him, I am the way, the truth, and the life: no man cometh unto*

the Father, but by me. If ye had known me, ye should have known my Father also: and from henceforth ye know him, and have seen him."

John 14:5-7 King James Version (KJV)

THIS ROAD CALLED LIFE

We know that our perfect life started and ended in the Garden of Eden. Certainly we know that Adam with the help of Eve was disobedient to God's instructions and sin entered the world. My Lord but how many of you know when there is active sin in your life it causes chaos and can wreak havoc. Adam's downfall created a life for us which is full of sin and degradation and the sad part about it is we did not even have a choice in the matter. One man's sin caused the whole entire world trouble and yet one man's (Jesus) obedience gave us back that life we lost. How amazing it is we never knew Adam but yet we inherited his sin and iniquities as soon as we were born. Funny how we not only inherited his wrongdoing but we also inherited the devil, who robbed him and us of our divine nature and privileges. Surely that was not God's intentions or desire for his children but one thing God gave man was free choice (free will) and until this day it has caused many men and women to fall prey to the enemies of life.

In the beginning was the Word, and the Word was with God, and the Word was God.

What do I mean by that? Let us take a look at "life" as we know it today. The world is in a saddened state everywhere you go there is danger seen and unseen, these days there is less God allowed and more violence present in homes, on jobs and my goodness even in elementary schools. It is almost as if sin has become the way of life. For example there is all types of abuse going on from physical, emotional, and mental abuse to fathers and mothers as well as adults having sex with their own children or someone else's children. My Lord, murder and suicides are increasing and Satan has the world believing it is okay to have sex with the same gender. Even the laws of the land are changing they have made it legal to marry the same sex but no law of the land can ever supersede God's law or God's hand of judgment.

The enemy of life looks like it has clearly taken over but I am here to tell you that God is still in control. Do not be fooled by what you see! Yes, the devil is very real and powerful in life but God is all powerful (omnipotent). Surely the enemy will receive his just reward in his due season. There is a scripture that pertains to this very thing and I want to use the Amplified version of Galatians 6:7 so that you can clearly understand what God is saying;

"Do not be deceived and deluded and misled; God will not allow Himself to be sneered at (scorned, disdained, or mocked by mere pretensions or professions, or by His precepts being set aside.) [He inevitably deludes himself who attempts to delude God.] For whatever a man sows, that and that only is what he will reap."

I use to believe that was an old cliché written and spoken by man then I found out it is the true word of God. Wow and I begin to realize that God's word does not fail or return unto Him void but it will truly accomplish that which he say. So two of the major factors in this road called life is: you reap what you sow and if God said it that settles it, and that there is true strategic revelation.

STRATEGY TO LIFE

"For I know that in me (that is, in my flesh,) dwelleth no good thing: for to will is present with me; but how to perform that which is good I find not. For the good that I would I do not: but the evil which I would not, that I do. Now if I do that I would not, it is no more I that do it, but sin that dwelleth in me. I find then a law, that, when I would do good, evil is present with me."

Romans 7:18-21 King James Version (KJV)

The strategy to life is; as we grow up we learn to war and choose between good and evil, good is always following us but yet evil is always present. See we were born with evil in us and so we have to work at being good until we discover the remedy to this situation, which is Jesus Christ. However, let's talk about the struggles that we wrestle with daily in this life for example fear, doubt, lack of self-esteem, lack of confidence in yourself, lack of trust, pride and let us not forget one, the biggest one of all self-centeredness. The reason why we have all these issues is because someone or something happened in our lives to trigger them. Surely the devil played a giant roll in planting these seeds in your life and storing them in your mind. So now I ask the question: what are you doing about these issues that you have developed while walking in this road we call life? I do not have to ask if you have them because everyone suffers or has to deal with one

> *The strategy to life is; as we grow up we learn to war and choose between good and evil.*

thing or the other because truly the Bible says that in this flesh dwells not one good thing. Now that is something to really ponder on. One of those things that make you go umm, because if not one thing in our flesh is good then how are we going to live a life that is pleasing to ourselves let alone God. Well this is why I am writing this book to let you know the strategies of life.

The Bible says when I was a child I thought as a child but when I grew up I put away childish things.

> *"When I was a child, I spake as a child, I understood as a child, I thought as a child: but when I became a man, I put away childish things. For now we see through a glass, darkly; but then face to face: now I know in part; but then shall I know even as also I am known."*
>
> *1 Corinthians 13:11-12 King James Version (KJV)*

This simply means at one time or another in my life I was not wise but may have been a little foolish and ignorant in the way I lived but now I have grown up and my thinking has matured. I was like a person in a dimly lit world because I had no knowledge of the spiritual world and no knowledge or very little knowledge of God. When you think about that it is kind of crazy, how do you not desire to get knowledge of whom you really are and who created you. I tell you how; it is not something that is taught in schools or your everyday life but it is taught in the church.

Here goes the problem with that if you do not go to church you may never learn about your creator until someone who is a Christian comes and introduces you to the Gospel and the other problem is people shy away from Christianity because of lack of knowledge and understanding.

"My people are destroyed for lack of knowledge: because thou hast rejected knowledge, I will also reject thee, that thou shalt be no priest to me: seeing thou hast forgotten the law of thy God, I will also forget thy children".

Hosea 4:6 King James Version (KJV)

They think they have to live a perfect life and the world gives a misconception that the Christians have no fun and are judgmental so they reject knowledge. Then what happens is their lack of knowledge does just what the devil wants it to do, deter them from the Gospel of Jesus Christ and sometimes the Christians behavior does not help it any. One thing that I have learned in this Christian walk is not to judge a book by its cover or its title but judge it by the content of its character. I also realize I need good character and a wealth of knowledge from God's word to help me overcome the pitfalls in life. I was only living from the physical aspect of life but had no knowledge of the spiritual so what would happen my lack of wisdom, knowledge and understanding gave the devil the upper hand in my life. Why? Because I did not understand that in real life there are two distinctive worlds; the seen (visible) and the unseen (invisible). There are the things that we can see visible with the naked eye and the things that exist in the spirit world which you can only see through spiritual eyes. This information alone gives you another strategy or strategic move to enhance your natural living as well as your spiritual living.

THE NATURAL LIFE VS. THE SPIRITUAL LIFE

"For our light affliction, which is but for a moment, worketh for us a far more exceeding and eternal weight of glory; While we look not at the things which are seen, but at the things which are not seen: for the things which are seen are temporal; but the things which are not seen are eternal."

2 Corinthians 4:17-18 King James Version (KJV)

When you think of natural life we are only here for a brief moment compared to spiritual life which will be an eternity. What we go through on earth is nothing compared to what we will go through in eternity when it comes to pain and suffering. Recognize that the scripture calls it our light affliction meaning it does not and cannot compare to the suffering that will go on in hell. We really never think about hell in terms of normal and natural living but understand this just as there is a God and a devil; there is a heaven and a hell. Do not be fooled by people or what you hear but read and study the Bible for yourself. It would be a sad situation for you to go to hell because you took the word of someone else over the word of God simply because you were too lazy to learn or look for yourself.

One of the greatest things I can teach you is don't let your laziness in your spiritual life cause you a natural disaster. What do I mean? Sometimes God will allow Satan to put trouble in your life so He can get your attention. It's not because he wants to hurt you but it is because God wants to help you get out the situation that you are in. Well if you are like me I thought I was good since my natural life was going great. I had no real relationship with God and had no idea that if I died I would have ended up in hell for eternity! I felt like I was living a good life, married and working hard yet staying out of trouble and had achieved a good career (a nurse) and acquired many material blessing. Little did I know I was on my road to hell because I lacked the knowledge of the Gospel and the knowledge of my Creator. My natural life was good, my family was well and all things seemed like they were on the right track until one day sickness hit our family.

Now here comes the part of the scripture that talks about the sickness that hit my family will: "*worketh for us a far more exceeding and eternal weight of glory.*" Little did we know God was setting us up for a miracle and a blessing at the same time but we could not see past the circumstance that we were being faced with. After all we had never had any real sickness or life threatening situations come this close to home and even worse right in our own house. Not that we had never experience sickness and death before in our family but it had been years and I guess you can say that we had forgotten or as they would say time heals all wounds. Well now this road we called life was beginning to take a turn and only God knows where it was going because we sure did not know. God has a way of getting your attention when you are not looking. Even though we had not chosen to serve Him, He had chose us and now it was time to give us a wakeup call.

After this real eye opener we realized we were missing something; yes we had natural gain but no spiritual life and no real relationship with our God.

"For what is a man profited, if he shall gain the whole world, and lose his own soul? or what shall a man give in exchange for his soul?"

Matthew 16:26 King James Version (KJV)

Funny how God works because surely we could not have obtained or attained anything we had if He had not given it to us. So yes we had prospered in this world and had not prepared for the eternal place of our soul because we were truly ignorant when it came to the afterlife, let alone the abundant life in Christ right here on earth. Many may have thought we were living the abundant life because to the eyes of this world we were. However to the eyes of the spirit we were not for surely we found out quickly that we are nothing without Jesus Christ!

What a way to find out that you are missing the greatest thing that can exist for a natural born human; a true relationship with your Creator, your Savior, your Redeemer, your Healer and your Deliverer. Well from that day forward I begin my quest to learn about my God. One thing I can say is that it woke up our entire household and we all went to church and gave our lives to the Lord. For surely what the devil meant for evil God turned it around for our good. I could not comprehend it then but truly I can comprehend it now! Surely I learned that there is no price or nothing that the devil can pay me for my soul or my life. I had now been introduced to a new way of life. Life as I knew it before was over I had found something new and they called it salvation and faith…. Hallelujah

> *"For I say, through the grace given unto me, to every man that is among you, not to think of himself more highly than he ought to think; but to think soberly, according as God hath dealt to every man the measure of faith."*
>
> (Romans 12:3 KJV)

I know it seems like faith should come first and it did but in my natural life I felt like salvation came first. However let me tell you there is a measure of faith given to you even to receive your salvation. It is just that you don't understand this at the time. You are just so excited that you have found God in the midst of what you been through. You do not even try to comprehend what is really going on because you are just so thankful the Lord brought you through it all. Then you look back and say my Lord what just happened in my life. I have just had my first known experience with God and it was fearful yet amazing but it leads me to my next encounter with Him salvation. Do I understand it all? Absolutely not but I am on my way to perfecting this life that I have been called into better known as Christianity or the Gospel of Jesus Christ. Now what's next?

SALVATION AND FAITH

> *"For I am not ashamed of the gospel of Christ: for it is the power of God unto salvation to every one that believeth; to the Jew first, and also to the Greek."*
>
> Romans 1:16 King James Version (KJV)

What is salvation and how do I receive it? Well to me receiving it was a whole lot easier than understanding it. Let us try to get an understanding of salvation first before we explain how you can receive it. Salvation if I put it in laymen's terms is a rescuing of yourself from sin, hell, Satan, death and anything that is contrary to God's will for your life. According to the Nelson New Illustrated Bible Dictionary *salvation is deliverance from the power of sin*. Let's go even further into that definition let's define the words deliverance and power. The word *deliverance* means an action of setting free or a rescue from moral corruption; now let us look at the word power. The word *power* means the possession of control or command over others; strength; might; force or rule. Oops, we have one more word that is of great importance that must be defined as well sin. What is sin? *Sin* is any serious offence, as against a religious or moral principle.

Now after defining all of these words and adding revelation from the Holy Spirit. Salvation can best be described as "the act of setting you free or rescuing you from the possession or control, strength and rule of any serious offence against God's divine and/or moral principles." I like to just make it simple and say we were rescue from the power of the devil's influence and force over our lives by Jesus Christ death and resurrection. Well I have given you many different analogies and explanations of what salvation means and is defined as. The reason I took so much time explaining it was because it is usually never really talked about that much in detail but mainly articulated as being saved or born again. Must I say being born again is once again the most important strategic move that you can ever make in life if we were playing chess this move would be considered checkmate.

Now before we get to check mate there are a few moves you need to make and let's look at a few scriptures that may help you. I personally like to look at the person of Nicodemus who was a well educated religious Jew but yet had no concept of what Jesus was talking about when He said you must be born again. The reason I like this particular character in the Bible because God makes two statements here you can be well educated in religious law, a teacher of the Law and not know who He is and also that some people will break the laws of religion to find Jesus. Nicodemus did both.

"There was a man of the Pharisees, named Nicodemus, a ruler of the Jews: The same came to Jesus by night, and said unto him, Rabbi, we know that thou art a teacher come from God: for no man can do these miracles that thou doest, except God be with him. Jesus answered and said unto him, Verily, verily, I say unto thee, Except a man be born again, he cannot see the kingdom of God."
John 3:1-3 King James Version (KJV)

Jesus meant that a natural man would not be able to understand or comprehend the Kingdom of God without a spiritual birth.

Now truly we all can understand that we are and was born in this life from our natural mother's womb but clearly that is not what Jesus is talking about. In case you do not know no one can save you but Jesus not your mother or father this is not a natural inheritance, salvation is a spiritual inheritance and rebirth.

> *"Be it known unto you all, and to all the people of Israel, that by the name of Jesus Christ of Nazareth, whom ye crucified, whom God raised from the dead, even by him doth this man stand here before you whole. This is the stone which was set at nought of you builders, which is become the head of the corner. Neither is there salvation in any other: for there is none other name under heaven given among men, whereby we must be saved."*
>
> Acts 4:10-12 King James Version (KJV).

As you read the Bible more and more you find out many were just like Nicodemus and also many rejected Jesus. Presently like Nicodemus many of us have these same questions he had but are afraid to ask or either can't understand what the Bible is saying.

So let's see what Jesus and Nicodemus has to teach us as we walk through this new road of life.

> *"Nicodemus saith unto him, How can a man be born when he is old? can he enter the second time into his mother's womb, and be born? Jesus answered, Verily, verily, I say unto thee, Except a man be born of water and of the Spirit, he cannot enter into the kingdom of God."*
>
> John 3:4-5 King James Version (KJV)

Jesus basically making it understood that being born of the water (natural birth) is not enough but you must be born of the spirit as well. One has no relationship to the other.

"That which is born of the flesh is flesh; and that which is born of the Spirit is spirit. Marvel not that I said unto thee, Ye must be born again. The wind bloweth where it listeth, and thou hearest the sound thereof, but canst not tell whence it cometh, and whither it goeth: so is every one that is born of the Spirit.."

John 3:6-8 King James Version (KJV)

Summing up this scripture as we have come to an end of Jesus explanation He says marvel not meaning don't be surprised just as it is impossible to explain the wind you will not be able to explain being born again in the spirit. Why? Plainly it is not to be understood intellectually but only can be understood spiritually.

Just as I have spoken earlier it is a lot easier to receive salvation than it is to explain it. For salvation comes through faith and confession. The word of the Lord explains it in Romans 10:8-10 King James Version (KJV)

"But what saith it? The word is nigh thee, even in thy mouth, and in thy heart: that is, the word of faith, which we preach; That if thou shalt confess with thy mouth the Lord Jesus, and shalt believe in thine heart that God hath raised him from the dead, thou shalt be saved. For with the heart man believeth unto righteousness; and with the mouth confession is made unto salvation."

The confession was the easy part; now let us talk about believing it; now that takes faith.

STRATEGIC FAITH

I pray by now that you understand the method to my madness as I give you the strategies of this road called "life" to get you to a place called victory. Now one thing about faith without it you cannot please God. However if you can master faith and seek after it diligently you will be rewarded by God.

"But without faith it is impossible to please him: for he that cometh to God must believe that he is, and that he is a rewarder of them that diligently seek him."
Hebrews 11:6 King James Version (KJV)

Now what must you first of all have faith for? You first and foremost must have faith to believe that He is God. It sounds very easy but in reality faith usually goes against all of the human laws that we have learned growing up. This is why we have so many different religions as well as atheist. People will believe in Buddha, Gandhi and all types of inanimate gods and statues because it is something that they can see and comprehend even if it doesn't make sense. However it is hard for many to believe in a God you cannot see or touch with the naked eye but yet is very much alive. Once again it can only be done by faith not academic or instructive means but this will only be done through a spiritual awakening in you and through you by God.

Let's look at the word faith. What does faith mean? Faith means confidence or trust in a person or thing, a strong and unshakeable belief in something esp. without no proof or evidence. The trust in God and in His promises as made through Christ and the Scriptures by which humans are justified or saved. Now let us look at what God said faith is.

WHAT IS FAITH?

ALL of God's people have the right to a dose of the anointing and faith, now how much you acquire will be solely up to you. For God's faith, power, and anointing is limitless and the more you hunger and thirst after righteousness the more you will be fed. It is never God's intention for us to go hungry or thirsty for anything. God is Jehovah Jireh, which means He is our provider and He shall and will supply all of our needs. As Christians we must develop our faith enough to believe that even in times of a drought or a struggle God will provide. Now what is faith and how do we get it?

"Now faith is the substance of things hoped for, the evidence of things not seen."

(Hebrews 11:1 KJV)

Faith is believing God for something you can't see, hear, or maybe not even understand. You truly have no way humanly possible of seeing it. It must be seen through the eyes of faith. Meaning neither the carnal mind nor the five senses can comprehend it (faith). Faith is just stepping out on God's word and guidance even when it doesn't make sense to our natural mind. Faith can get you things from God that hard work could never get you. For through faith we can move mountains and obtain blessings and promises that only can be given to you by God. God is the only one who has the power and the ability to bypass the natural recommendations and/or requirements. See faith is the blessed hope and the sure knowledge that God is able to do everything but fail and nothing is impossible for Him. (Hallelujah!)

To understand faith you must get to know God for Jesus was the epitome of faith. Jesus is our true and living example of faith. He trusted and believed in all God's promises, blessings, commands, and statues. He never wavered in anything that the Father said to Him; for He trusted wholly and completely in everything the Father said. Why did He trust the Father simply put in the words of Jesus "For I and the Father are one, if you have seen me then you have seen the Father." See faith and the Trinity (The Father, The Son, and The Holy Spirit) are truly the mysteries of the Bible. You can't see them with your natural eyes but surely you know that they exist.

So now we are ready for our next question. What I like about God is He does not leave you ignorant as to how to obtain or attain anything from Him but He puts it in His Bible which is our basic life instructions. How do I get faith?

HOW DO WE GET FAITH?

How do we get faith? "So then faith cometh by hearing, and hearing by the word of God." (Romans 10:17 KJV) Now we just learned what faith is and now here in this scripture God has given us an answer to our question. So faith comes by hearing now let us look at the word hearing. Hearings definition is the sense by which sound is perceived; the capacity to hear. Now let us look at the word hear which is the verb. Hear means to perceive sound by the ear but let's go a little further into the definition it also means to listen to attentively, to learn by hearing; be told by others, to receive news or information; learn. These extensive definitions take you to another place and give you a lot more detail on how to receive faith. It goes much further than just hearing the word of God through the audible sound.

Not only must you hear it through your natural ear but also you must listen attentively and learn. See faith comes by learning God's word (The Bible), attentively listening, and paying close attention to detail. As we read Romans 10:17 and did a little research and expounding we found out that the word of God is not always as simple as it may sound. However to get full understanding of God's word we must pray, read other scriptures, and look up some vocabulary words in the dictionary. We must go to all lengths to get a good revelation (supernatural or divine meaning) of the word of God. The more we know and understand the more our faith increases.

The more your faith increases the more you began to exercise God's principles in your life. This is when you can become a doer of the word not just a hearer. Now remember we just learned that a hearer was a person who paid close attention to God's word and learned it. Now you have moved on to the next level for you are now performing that which you have just learned. You have learned about salvation and faith and recognize that it is your choice if you want to adhere to the word of the Lord or not. You also will have to learn how to walk out and work out your own soul salvation with fear and trembling but without murmuring and complaining about what curveballs life has thrown you. We cannot change anything from the past all we can do now is work our faith, be odebient, and believe that Jesus Christ is still in control of all things in heaven and under the earth.

> *"That at the name of Jesus every knee should bow, of things in heaven, and things in earth, and things under the earth; And that every tongue should confess that Jesus Christ is Lord, to the glory of God the Father. Wherefore, my beloved, as ye have always obeyed, not as in my presence only, but now much more in my absence, work out your own salvation with fear and trembling. For it is God which worketh in you both to will and to do of his good pleasure. Do all things without murmurings and disputing."*
> *Philippians 2:10-14 King James Version (KJV)*

Now that we have learned two of the most important strategic divine principles in life which is faith and salvation we must hold fast to what we have read and learned. No matter how our life ends up we must believe that God can and will turn everything around for our good. Is life always going to be a fairy tale and will all dreams come true? Of course not but we must hold onto our faith without wavering and encourage one another as we go through our good times as well as our trials and tribulations. We must assemble ourselves together in church meeting or at home as we show love, do good works and help one another in all things which is God's desire for his children.

> *"Let us hold fast the profession of our faith without wavering; (for he is faithful that promised ;) And let us consider one*

another to provoke unto love and to good works: Not forsaking the assembling of ourselves together, as the manner of some is; but exhorting one another: and so much the more, as ye see the day approaching."

Hebrews 10:23-25
King James Version (KJV)

Currently as we close out the faith and salvation section I want to talk about something that is just as important. Let's talk about our basic life necessities that we as humans need. If we do not receive them in this life it could cause us to become depressed, lose our minds, or maybe even become sick and/or die naturally or spiritually.

BASIC LIFE INSTRUCTIONS

"For God so loved the world, that he gave his only begotten Son, that whosoever believeth in him should not perish, but have everlasting life. For God sent not his Son into the world to condemn the world; but that the world through him might be saved."

John 3:16-17 King James Version (KJV)

There are some basic things that you need to survive in this life naturally and spiritually. According to Maslow's Hierarchy and the Bible love is one of our greatest needs as well as safety and belonging. How many of you know our whole life is based on love. God loved us so much that He sent His only begotten son to die for us. I also know according to human growth and development without love you cannot live a healthy and normal life. There are many different types of love but all love should be beneficial to you and if it is not beneficial to your mind, body and spirit then we have to determine if it is really love. My main concern moreover is whether or not you have love because if you have not love you definitely don't have God dwelling in you.

> *"He that loveth not knoweth not God; for God is love. In this was manifested the love of God toward us, because that God sent his only begotten Son into the world, that we might live through him. Herein is love, not that we loved God, but that he loved us, and sent his Son to be the propitiation for our sins."*
>
> 1 John 4:8-10 King James Version (KJV)

WHAT IS LOVE?

Love is defined as a strong affection for another arising out of kinship or personal ties, attraction based on sexual desire : affection and tenderness felt by lovers, affection based on admiration, benevolence, or common interests, unselfish loyal and benevolent concern for the good of another: as: brotherly concern for others, the fatherly concern of God for humankind. Now when we look at the Nelson's Bible Dictionary love is the high esteem that God has for His human children and the high regard which they in turn should have for Him and other people. Love is one of God's attribute; it is also an essential part of His nature. God is the epitome of love. Let's look at what God says about love in the scriptures.

One thing God speaks about is being rooted in grounded in love this in return will help the saints understand the depth and the magnitude of His love. It can only come by being strengthened with might by God's spirit through your inner man. Man really cannot comprehend this kind of love on his own it has to come through Christ because it surpasses our human knowledge. Love comes when Christ dwells in your heart through faith, then and only then can He grant you according to the riches of His glory that ye might be filled with all the fullness of God.

> *"That he would grant you, according to the riches of his glory, to be strengthened with might by his Spirit in the inner man; That Christ may dwell in your hearts by faith; that ye, being rooted and grounded in love, May be able to comprehend with all saints what is the breadth, and length, and depth, and height; And to know the love of Christ, which passeth knowledge, that ye might be filled with all the fulness of God."*
> *Ephesians 3:16-19 King James Version (KJV)*

Let's look at another one of the scriptures which teaches us about love:

> *"And though I bestow all my goods to feed the poor, and though I give my body to be burned, and have not charity, it profiteth me nothing. Charity suffereth long, and is kind; charity envieth not; charity vaunteth not itself, is not puffed up, Doth not behave itself unseemly, seeketh not her own, is not easily provoked, thinketh no evil; Rejoiceth not in iniq-*

uity, but rejoiceth in the truth; Beareth all things, believeth all things, hopeth all things, endureth all things.

1 Corinthians 13:3-7
King James Version (KJV)

This scripture let's you discern it does not matter how morally good you are and how great you can operate in the natural world or spiritual world without love you are nothing. To make it plain and simple love is not puffed up, nor envious, nor seeks to do harm or evil, and definitely does not rejoice in your sins but it bears all things and endures all things and suffers long. It does not mean that you become a fool for love but it also does not mean that you make a fool of someone who loves you either. One thing I do know God's love never fails and His love covered a multitude of our sins actually His love covered all of our sins through the shedding of His blood. This will lead me to inform you of the next part of life's strategy, called safety and belonging.

SAFETY AND BELONGING

When we talk about safety and belonging it is a great requirement of this road called life. Everyone wants to feel loved, needed and safe. If one of them is missing in your life it can cause you to have a bad experience. Belonging is characterized by having a place that you can call your own, a place where you fit in per se. Without a sense of belonging, a person grows up feeling lonely, empty and not loved developing what we call today low self esteem. As people we belong to churches, families and organizations but are they being effective in our lives or are we just coping with where we have landed. Some of us have learned to fit in where people allow us to get in; instead of picking and choosing our places, friends and churches according to moral and/or divine standards.

Relationships are a necessity and a vital part of our life but we must be careful and prayerful who we choose to allow in our personal, emotional, physical and spiritual atmosphere. We are supposed to have a multitude of relationships in our lives this gives us a sense of purpose as well as freedom to be who we are in life. When we have a sense of purpose and freedom it also gives us a feeling of safety. I want you to realize that when you belong to someone, something or God it is a sense of security and acceptance. Feeling accepted gives us confidence to share our thoughts and feelings without being rejected or treated bad. Let me give you a few examples: people join gangs among many other organizations because they are looking for a place to belong, many husbands and wives have extra marital affairs because they feel rejected, unloved or married but neglected and I could go on and on with many others but I think you get the picture. Before you attempt to help someone else make sure you examine yourself and whatever you find that is lacking NOW is a good time to fix it. Once again what I love about God he knew before the foundation of the world we would need help in all areas of our lives so He sent the third person of the Godhead called the Holy Spirit to help us. I call Him the Helper of Life.

THE HELPER OF LIFE

"Nevertheless I tell you the truth; It is expedient for you that I go away: for if I go not away, the Comforter will not come unto you; but if I depart, I will send him unto you."

John 16:7 King James Version (KJV)

The helper of life is the greatest thing that you can learn about better known as the Holy Spirit. Jesus after completing His work on the earth spoke to His disciples and let them know that it is expedient that He leave so he can send you a Comforter that will help you and guide you in all things. This is what I call the ultimate helper because the Holy Spirit knows all things, and is given instructions from God himself and is also God himself. This is truly one of the mysteries of the Bible.

"But the Comforter, which is the Holy Ghost, whom the Father will send in my name, he shall teach you all things, and bring all things to your remembrance, whatsoever I have said unto you."

John 14:26 King James Version (KJV)

Although it may be one of our greatest mysteries but it is not mystical (magical)…

There is truly a big difference in those two. The Holy Spirit is our lifeline when it comes to needing natural and spiritual guidance. He not only will tell you the truth about life but He will also testify the truth about Jesus Christ.

> *"But when the Comforter is come, whom I will send unto you from the Father, even the Spirit of truth, which proceedeth from the Father, he shall testify of me."*
>
> *John 15:26 King James Version (KJV)*

God the Father gives us many commandments and statues but the Holy Spirit is the person of the Godhead that helps us to carry out God's instructions. Here is an interesting but vital scripture that is an example of what the Holy Ghost can help us to do. The Holy Ghost will allow us to keep God's commandments when He abides in us.

> *"If ye love me, keep my commandments. And I will pray the Father, and he shall give you another Comforter, that he may abide with you for ever; Even the Spirit of truth; whom the world cannot receive, because it seeth him not, neither knoweth him: but ye know him; for he dwelleth with you, and shall be in you."*
>
> *John 14:15-17 King James Version (KJV)*

Now as I come to the close of chapter one which I called "Strategic" I want to make sure you understand the method behind the madness before we move on to warfare. Well in Chapter one I told you the main points, emotions, issues and ideas that will cause you to either win the war or lose it. I pray that you understand that everything I spoke about in this chapter is your route to a successful and an abundant life in Christ if it is learned and applied correctly. When you look at something strategically that means you are setting up a plan to win or defeat someone or get the victory over something. Well in this book you will learn the Lord's plan for victory over every situation in your life and we will accomplish it through our wisdom, knowledge and understanding of who God is, what Jesus has done, and last but not least receiving and using the power of the Holy Spirit.

Warfare

*"And the LORD God said unto the serpent, Because thou hast done this, **thou art cursed above** all cattle, and above every beast of the field; upon thy belly shalt thou go, and dust shalt thou eat all the days of thy life: **And I will put enmity between thee and the woman, and between thy seed and her seed;** it shall bruise thy head, and thou shalt bruise his heel."*

Genesis 3:14-15 KJV

My Lord sometimes we embark on things in life and never really understand where it came from, why is it in my life or how do I get rid of it. Well let us talk a little bit about warfare and where it came from. Warfare came into the world from two distinct events the serpent tricked Eve which in turn influenced Adam to be disobedient to God's instructions. This disobedience from Adam and the craftiness of the serpent caused the Lord to put enmity between the woman's seed which is mankind and the serpent's seed. In other words they would always be enemies in natural life and as we grow in the spirit we find out that we have a spiritual enemy as well called Satan. Enmity means hostile towards one another and hatred for one another. Here is where we see the beginning of conflict and warfare in life as we know it.

The second incident is when Satan got kicked out of heaven for trying to be like God.

> *For thou hast said in thine heart, I will ascend into heaven, I will exalt my throne above the stars of God: I will sit also upon the mount of the congregation, in the sides of the north: I will ascend above the heights of the clouds; I will be like the most High."*
>
> *Isaiah 14:13-14 KJV*

Surely Satan must have known he could not be the Creator when he himself was the creation. What would make him think he could be like the Most High when he was created as an angelic being? Sometimes in this road called life the devil can play tricks on you so he can deceive you. What I found out about Satan is he is such a good deceiver he even deceived himself into believing he could be like God. Now I truly understand why he is called a deceiver and the Father of Lies….He does it so well he destroyed himself and now his desire is to destroy us right along with him. My job in this book is to make sure you don't allow him to destroy you and that you are made aware of who he is and what is his purpose on this earth as well as in the realm of the spirit. Well let us take a look at what the Bible says about this:

Many Christians are not familiar with spiritual warfare.

"The thief cometh not, but for to steal, and to kill, and to destroy: I am come that they might have life, and that they might have it more abundantly."

John 10:10 (King James Version)

In case you do not know, this scripture informs you that the thief (which is Satan) comes to steal your hopes and dreams, kill your spiritual destiny and destroy everything that is connected to your life. Now that is the negative side of the outcome of life. Oh but we have another alternative to this that gives us the ultimate victory in this life and his name is Jesus. Jesus came so that we may have life (natural, emotional, physical and spiritual wholeness and peace) and have it more abundantly (until it overflows). See faith in Jesus is the beginning strategy and the answer to overcoming Satan plans. Once you realize who Jesus is and who Satan is you have won half the battle. Now the other half of the battle will come when you recognize that God is greater than anything the devil can throw at you. Once you realize who is who and that our weapons are not carnal (fleshly) but they are spiritual your whole strategy changes. "For the weapons of our warfare are not carnal, but mighty through God to the pulling down of strong *holds;) Casting down imaginations, and every high thing that exalteth itself against the knowledge of God, and bringing into captivity every thought to the obedience of Christ." Corinthians 10:4-7 King James Version (KJV)*

> Satan uses people, situation and circumstances to get his work done while he hides behind the plan.

People are familiar with the scriptures of the Bible but do they have true revelation and illumination of what God is trying to reveal and unveil to His people. The Lord let us know do not attempt to fight your enemy with flesh for you can never beat Satan through your flesh or physically. Why? Truly because Satan is a spiritual being a fallen angel and he has a spiritual army of fallen angels better known to us as demonic angelic hosts. In order to win this battle you will have to change your thinking and cast down some imaginations and some high thoughts that you have learned in your normal life. Many in natural life are afraid of the devil but those who understand the power of God and salvation surely are not afraid of anything that is demonic.

One our many lessons in life are to recognize who is your enemy and believe it or not we all have the same enemy our flesh and Satan also better known as the devil. Many of us think of people as being our enemies and it is true to a certain extent. Being that Satan is a spiritual being he needs to use a human mind and body to operate in. The key to your success in warfare is to make sure that Satan is not using you. Once you understand who Satan is and what his purpose is, it becomes a lot easier to discern his schemes and plans! One of the downfalls of the Christian is they teach the people about God but they do not teach people about the devil. Yes, it is true God is in control of the world but Satan is also very active in this present world as well. Let's take a look at the mind of Satan.

MASTERMIND OF SATAN

"How art thou fallen from heaven, O Lucifer, son of the *morning! how art thou cut down to the ground, which didst weaken the nations!" Isaiah 14:12 KJV*

This chapter will inform you of who Satan is and what his plan for your life is. Trust me Satan's plan and God's plan are total opposites. Satan wants you to end up in the very pit of hell and God wants you to join Him in heaven. Now the funny thing about all of this is; the choice is entirely up to you. So my job as an author is to inform you and empower you to make the right choice which of course is heaven. However in order to make the right choice you need to know the mastermind of Satan and develop the mind of Christ to beat the devil at his own game. Satan is the mastermind behind everything that is demonic and everything pertaining to anything that is against God's Word, His Nature, or His Will.

What do I mean by the mastermind? When you look the word mastermind up in the dictionary it means "a person who plans and supervises a scheme or operation usually behind the scenes or to devise and conduct a plan of action, usually behind the scenes." In other words Satan uses people, situation and circumstances to get his work done while he hides behind the plan. In other words he has a plan of destruction against the life of the Christian but his job is to be so good at the plan of destruction that you never recognize that it was the devil.

His entire job is to make sure all mankind ends up in the very pits of hell because that is truly his destination. Many of us do not realize that Satan's job is to steal, kill and destroy that which God has created. So our job as the Body of Christ is to have the mind of Christ and eradicate the plans of Satan by exposing them.

THE MIND OF CHRIST

> *"Look not every man on his own things, but every man also on the things of others. Let this mind be in you, which was also in Christ Jesus: Who, being in the form of God, thought it not robbery to be equal with God: But made himself of no reputation, and took upon him the form of a servant, and was made in the likeness of men: And being found in fashion*

as a man, he humbled himself, and became obedient unto death, even the death of the cross."
Philippians 2:4-8 King James Version (KJV)

What exactly does having the mind of Christ entail? Well let us look at who Christ is notice that it says the mind of Christ. The word Christ means the anointed one. So the first thing I think of is having the anointed mind of Jesus. Wow, now can you really comprehend having the mind of Jesus let alone it is anointed by the Holy Spirit that's like carrying a double barrel shot gun in the spirit. God is all knowing and if you can catch by faith the mind of Christ you yourself can become a wise and dangerous servant of the Lord and for the Lord. In other words an anointed mind of Christ has the power and the ability to destroy every yoke that is presented in the natural and in the spirit. If you want to have the mind of Christ now you also have to think like Christ which means it is not about you (no reputation) and that you should be willing to be obedient to God even if it kills you. Believe me not many can humble themselves to this level let alone become a servant or a slave to Christ. Actually it will take an anointed mind of Christ to do this.

But he that is spiritual judgeth all things, yet he himself is judged of no man. For who hath known the mind of the Lord, that he may instruct him? but we have the mind of Christ.
1 Corinthians 2:15-16 King James Version (KJV

Walking in this kind of anointing takes a lot of faith, divine knowledge and wisdom. It is definitely easier said than done but if you desire to win the war against Satan, having the mind of Christ will certainly have to become a reality to you. The mind of Christ also helps us to get revelation of His word (which is also considered to be God's thoughts or instructions) and also teaches us not to be ignorant of the devices of the enemies. *"Lest Satan should get an advantage of us: for we are not ignorant of his devices." 2 Corinthians 2:11 (KJV)*

Now let's look at some of the enemies in our lives.

ENEMIES OF LIFE

"And they overcame him by the blood of the Lamb, and by the word of their testimony; and they loved not their lives unto the death. Therefore rejoice, ye heavens, and ye that dwell in them. Woe to the inhabiters of the earth and of the sea! for the devil is come down unto you, having great wrath, because he knoweth that he hath but a short time."

Revelation 12:11-12
King James Version (KJV)

When you talk about the enemies of life it can include many things I am going to touch on the most common ones and let you know that you have victory over them through the blood of the Lamb and the word of your testimony**.** The devil knows that he only has a short time so he throws at you everything he can think of. His job is to find your weakness in your flesh. Your job is to know your strength is in God. Though we can never be perfect and will fall short of the glory of God we don't have to fall prey to Satan continuously. All we have to do is find the solution in the Bible to that enemy in your life that has got you bound and apply it to your life. Now there are many different ways in the word of God to combat the enemies of life but the first thing we must do is admit the problem and seek help.

THE SPIRIT OF FEAR

What a lot of people do not recognize is the everyday enemies that keep you locked up for years for example fear. There is good fear and then there is fear that cripples us and paralyzes us. What we must know is the crippling fear is of the devil. What exactly is fear? Fear is defined as a feeling of agitation and/or anxiety caused by present or imminent danger; a feeling of disquiet or apprehension; extreme reverence or awe as toward a deity. When we look at the definition we can honestly say that everyone has or have had some fear in their lives but faith is the solution to fear. This is probably one of the greatest enemies man faces daily. We are afraid of failure, success, people, the devil and sometimes we even fear ourselves. The Lord knows fear is such a great enemy of faith that throughout the Bible God told His people continuously fear not for I am with you. One thing I know for sure if God be for you who can be against you. So I leave you with these two scriptures to combat your fear.

"So that we may boldly say, The Lord is my helper, and I will not fear what man shall do unto me."
Hebrews 13:6 King James Version (KJV)

"For God hath not given us the spirit of fear; but of power, and of love, and of a sound mind."
2 Timothy 1:7 King James Version (KJV)

THE SPIRIT OF LACK OF SUBMISSION

Once again this is one of the tactics the enemy uses against you so that you either wind up being rebellious or disobedient; either way Satan gets the victory. In this world we must learn to submit to authority whether it is your natural parents, spiritual parents, husband, wife, the government, the law or God himself. Many are out of the will of God because they will not submit to His authority and many are out of jobs because they cannot submit to their boss or the rules on a job. On the other hand many are locked up in prison because they grew up refusing to submit to the laws of the land. God put rule over you and rules over the land and when you do not follow them there are repercussions and truly all of us can look back over our lives and pinpoint a place where we failed in this area one time or another. I tell you this because if you want to win this war against the devil and walk in victory in this life and the life to come you surely have to learn to surrender. Just so you comprehend what I am talking about here is the definition of *Lack of Submission*- the act of not submitting (yielding or surrender) to the power of another; the state of being non-compliant. Once again here is what the Lord's word has to say about this enemy in the camp.

"Obey them that have the rule over you, and submit yourselves: for they watch for your souls, as they that must give account, that they may do it with joy, and not with grief: for that is unprofitable for you."

Hebrews 13:17 King James Version (KJV)

"Submit yourselves therefore to God. Resist the devil, and he will flee from you. Draw nigh to God, and he will draw nigh to you. Cleanse your hands, ye sinners; and purify your hearts, ye double minded."

James 4:7-8 King James Version (KJV)

"Submitting yourselves one to another in the fear of God. Wives, submit yourselves unto your own husbands, as unto the Lord. For the husband is the head of the wife, even as Christ is the head of the church: and he is the saviour of the body. Therefore as the church is subject unto Christ, so let the wives be to their own husbands in every thing. Husbands, love your wives, even as Christ also loved the church, and gave himself for it."

Ephesians 5:21-25 King James Version (KJV)

THE SPIRIT OF PRIDE

Well well well…this is the one no one likes to admit but it is visible to the devil because truly pride is what caused him to fall. Pride is a sense of one's own proper dignity or value; self-respect; pleasure or satisfaction taken in an achievement, a possession, or an association; arrogant or disdainful conduct or treatment; haughtiness. Surely you know like anything else there is good and bad in everything. The good pride is not considered your enemy so let us look at the pride that comes before the fall. Surely we are talking about the arrogance and haughtiness of a person who thinks more highly of themselves and their achievements then they ought to. This kind of person likes to project a spirit that will make you feel less than or lower than and spews a spirit of rejection if they feel you are not on their level. The solution to this enemy is to first recognize you are nothing without God and everything you have achieved or own is because God allowed it. So how dare you put your nose up at anyone when God was your source and not you yourself? Now learn to humble yourself before Satan helps you self-destruct. Here are a few scriptures for you to meditate on.

> *See many confess that they know God and are his children but your ways sometimes will speak louder than your praise.*

"Pride goeth before destruction, and an haughty spirit before a fall. Better it is to be of an humble spirit with the lowly, than to divide the spoil with the proud."

Proverbs 16:18-19 King James Version (KJV)

"For if a man know not how to rule his own house, how shall he take care of the church of God?) Not a novice, lest being lifted up with pride he fall into the condemnation of the devil."

1 Timothy 3:5-6 King James Version (KJV)

"A man's pride shall bring him low: but honour shall uphold the humble in spirit."

Proverbs 29:23 King James Version (KJV)

THE SPIRIT OF SELFISHNESS/DISOBEDIENCE

I personally tied these two together because one causes the other. If you are selfish then everything you do will be to please yourself and I know according to the word of God that is the reason many of us sin. Sin entered the world through disobedience and selfishness and after Adam sinned against God he blamed it on the woman God had given him. He sinned because he did not listen to what the Lord had told him but he listened to Eve. One man selfishness and disobedience caused a world to fall into sin and one man's obedience shall many be made righteous. *Selfishness* is concerned chiefly and only with oneself and *Disobedience* is refusal or failure to obey. Satisfying your flesh will cause you to become disobedient to God's will and His ways. Most of the sins in this world come from man's attempt to satisfy his flesh for example prostitution, pornography, sexual and physical abuse, lying, stealing, adultery, fornication, gossiping and all types of addictions. I am not only talking about the world but this is also very present in the saints. They have found God and received salvation but have not renewed their mind, changed their character or their ways.

See many confess that they know God and are his children but your ways sometimes will speak louder than your praise. In this season make a promise to yourself that you will put God first and God will send the Holy Spirit to help you with your selfishness and disobedience. Examine yourself and find out is your selfishness causing you to sin and miss out on the blessings God has for you. Here are some scriptures that can affirm that which I have said.

"For as by one man's disobedience many were made sinners, so by the obedience of one shall many be made righteous."
Romans 5:19 King James Version (KJV)

"They profess that they know God; but in works they deny him, being abominable, and disobedient, and unto every good work reprobate."
Titus 1:16 KJV King James Version (KJV)

"For we ourselves also were sometimes foolish, disobedient, deceived, serving divers lusts and pleasures, living in malice and envy, hateful, and hating one another. But after that the kindness and love of God our Saviour toward man appeared.
Titus 3:3-5 King James Version (KJV)

THE SPIRIT OF COVETOUSNESS

This sin is so prevalent that it is one of the Ten Commandments. We see so many people fall into this sin in this world by trying to keep up with the Joneses. Covetousness is defined as excessively and culpably desirous of possessions of another. A great example of this in the Bible is David going after Bathsheba and as much as David loved God he still was coveting another man's wife. We see this in the government; we see this in business deals, we see this in church's as well. How many times do we see someone establish a company, business or a church and another man desires it and tries to take it over or take it from them. When it is accomplished in the realm of the spirit or in the natural we call it a hostile takeover.

You took something that does not belong to you and that's a sign that sin has penetrated in your heart but manifested in the natural life. Watch out that this sin does not sneak up on you just as it did David. Be careful when you have a strong desire for someone else's possessions or mates, that is a warning sign that you are heading in the wrong direction and looking for trouble and Satan will surely help you find it. So if you think this maybe one of your enemies here are a few scriptures to tell you what God thinks about this sin.

"The prince that wanteth understanding is also a great oppressor: but he that hateth covetousness shall prolong his days."
Proverbs 28:16 King James Version (KJV)

"And he said, That which cometh out of the man, that defileth the man. For from within, out of the heart of men, proceed evil thoughts, adulteries, fornications, murders, Thefts, covetousness, wickedness, deceit, lasciviousness, an evil eye, blasphemy, pride, foolishness: All these evil things come from within, and defile the man."
Mark 7:20-23 King James Version (KJV)

"And he said unto them, Take heed, and beware of covetousness: for a man's life consisteth not in the abundance of the things which he possesseth."
Luke 12:15 King James Version (KJV)

"Let your conversation be without covetousness; and be content with such things as ye have: for he hath said, I will never leave thee, nor forsake thee."

Hebrews 13:5 King James Version (KJV)

THE SPIRIT OF LASCIVIOUSNESS

This sin has caused the world to change the laws of the land. We have men lusting after men and women lusting after women and the government saying it is alright to marry one another. Parents are lusting after their own children and grown-ups desiring to have sex with children and watching lewd sexual acts on computers. Lord help us what is the world coming to? *Lasciviousness* is defined as given to or expression of lust; exciting sexual desires; lustful. As if prostitution and pornography wasn't enough now this has truly gotten out of hand. Man's lustful desires have almost made the world believe this behavior is acceptable. It maybe to the world but it is certainly not acceptable to God.

Some of this behavior may have come from generational curses, an impartation or transference but wherever it comes from we know for sure it is truly of the devil. Yes sin comes from many different sources and ways. That's why the Lord speaks in His word to lay hands on no man suddenly which in turn means do not allow everyone to lay hands on you suddenly either. These spirits are definitely transferable and can cause you to fall into sin and make a mess out of your life. This is very real it is nothing to play with. It is sin that causes man's demise and death and the sad part is it primarily comes from a lack of knowledge. Here again is a little help for you;

"And lest, when I come again, my God will humble me among you, and that I shall bewail many which have sinned already, and have not repented of the uncleanness and fornication and lasciviousness which they have committed."
2 Corinthians 12:21 King James Version (KJV)

"Having the understanding darkened, being alienated from the life of God through the ignorance that is in them, because of the blindness of their heart: Who being past feeling have given themselves over unto lasciviousness, to work all uncleanness with greediness. But ye have not so learned Christ; If so be that ye have heard him, and have been taught by him, as the truth is in Jesus."
Ephesians 4:18-21 King James Version (KJV)

"That he no longer should live the rest of his time in the flesh to the lusts of men, but to the will of God. For the time past of our life may suffice us to have wrought the will of the Gentiles, when we walked in lasciviousness, lusts, excess of wine, revellings, banquetings, and abominable idolatries."
1 Peter 4:2-3 King James Version (KJV)

THE SPIRIT OF JEALOUSY

Jealousy is what the world says, is bad to the bone. Jealousy will cause men to kill, steal, hurt and maybe even try to destroy a person and their character. Just like some of the other enemies of life there is a jealousy that will try to destroy and then there is a jealousy that God has for his children. God does not desire you to love anything or anyone more than Him. He must be first in your life. However there is another form of jealousy that is dangerous to the human species and it causes resentment and bitterness towards a person or rivalry. This spirit is very prevalent in the world and the church. We find people betraying and backbiting one another because of the spirit of jealousy. Jealousy is defined as resentful or bitter in rivalry; envious; fearful or wary of being supplanted; apprehensive of losing affection or position; closely vigilante. Throughout the Bible we have read many stories that pertain or are caused because of the spirit of jealousy. Let us look at Cain and Abel the first murder recorded in the Bible was because of jealousy and envy. Lord help is truly needed from the Holy Spirit for those who are carriers or influence by this spirit for it can cause rage and a man will wreak havoc in the life of himself and his rival.

> *"For jealousy is the rage of a man: therefore he will not spare in the day of vengeance."*
> *Proverbs 6:34 King James Version (KJV)*

> *"Set me as a seal upon thine heart, as a seal upon thine arm: for love is strong as death; jealousy is cruel as the grave: the coals thereof are coals of fire, which hath a most vehement flame."*
> *Song of Solomon 8:6 King James Version (KJV)*

"For I am jealous over you with godly jealousy: for I have espoused you to one husband, that I may present you as a chaste virgin to Christ."
2 Corinthians 11:2 King James Version (KJV)

THE SPIRIT OF ENVY

This spirit is worse than jealousy because it causes the person to have hatred and ill will towards you because of your advantages or possessions. Notice God's word said jealousy was as cruel as the grave but according to the word envy is like rottenness to the bones. This is some way to describe these two spirits jealousy will cause you to envy if it is not dealt with. This spirit will cause you to rot and miss out on what God has for you as you resent the possessions of someone else.

Envy is defined as a feeling of discontent and resentment aroused by desire for possessions or qualities of another. To envy someone is to feel ill will, jealousy, or discontent at his possession of something that one keenly desires to have or achieve oneself. Notice jealousy is included in this because it is the root cause and festered until it became a stronger spirit. Be very careful of the spirit of jealousy, covetousness and envy the all will cause you to lose sight of your purpose because you are focused on someone else's achievements, money, ministry, mate or material gains. Just keep your eyes on God and He will give you the desires of your heart if you walk upright. The Lord said no good thing will he uphold from you if you seek him correctly and with the right motive. Do not let envy be a reason for your destruction. Pray and release yourself from this spirit as we look at what God has to say about the spirit of envy.

> *"For wrath killeth the foolish man, and envy slayeth the silly one."*
> *Job 5:2 King James Version (KJV)*

> *"Envy thou not the oppressor, and choose none of his ways."*
> *Proverbs 3:31 King James Version (KJV)*

> *"A sound heart is the life of the flesh: but envy the rottenness of the bones."*
> *Proverbs 14:30 King James Version (KJV)*

> *"For I fear, lest, when I come, I shall not find you such as I would, and that I shall be found unto you such as ye would not: lest there be debates, envyings, wraths, strifes, backbitings, whisperings, swellings, tumults."*
> *2 Corinthians 12:20 King James Version (KJV)*

THE SPIRIT OF STRIFE

My Lord this a combative spirit ruled by anger, jealousy, envy and more than likely listening to gossiping folks who do not have your best interest at heart. They are usually putting fuel to the fire because this is a spirit that is visible to the naked eye and audible to the natural ear. Strife is defined as a heated, often violent dissension; bitter conflict; a struggle, fight, or quarrel; contention or competition between rivals. You find this in the church a lot and it is very slick and crafty if you are not careful. It is the person who is giving you all the negative information from another person and causing you to dislike your leaders or those who desire to help you in the spirit. See their goal is to cause strife in the church and in your life so you can abort your purpose and miss your destiny. Stay clear of a person who is always causing dissension in the church, speaking negative about the same person, or dropping seeds of discord which makes you angry at another person.

In this season judge for yourself and unless you hear it with your own ears be very careful; remember Satan is a liar and a great deceiver and if you are not careful the devil will use you like a pawn. I have seen this spirit transferred so much in the church via gossip and many have fallen and never even realized what happened to them. Next thing they know they are arguing and fighting at work, at home or in the church because the spirit of strife has taken root in their hearts, mind and spirit. Lord knows we want fire in our churches and our homes but not this kind of fire. We want God's consuming fire that will eradicate this spirit and expose it and the person who fuels it. Once again examine yourself and if this spirit is present in your life, your home or your church ask the Lord to eradicate it and expose it to you. Let's look at what the word of the Lord says about strife:

> *"A wrathful man stirreth up strife: but he that is slow to anger appeaseth strife."*
>
> *Proverbs 15:18 King James Version (KJV)*

"He loveth transgression that loveth strife: and he that exalteth his gate seeketh destruction."
                    Proverbs 17:19 King James Version (KJV)

"An angry man stirreth up strife, and a furious man aboundeth in transgression."
                    Proverbs 29:22 King James Version (KJV)

THE SPIRIT OF GOSSIP

This is a spirit that fuels all the other spirits that I have talked about. Gossip will make you fear people, cause you shame and will make you regress. Many people have been hurt by gossip and sometimes it can even destroy people's lives. When we look at the world it loves sin and what better way to sin than to talk about another man and his problems in the open rather than help him in private. Gossip is also another way of trying to hold you back or persecute you. Surely this is an age old sin and it will always be around just like the poor. Gossip is defined as rumors or talks of a personal, sensational, or intimate nature; a person who habitually spreads rumors; trivial, chatty talk. One thing about a gossiper the person also usually has the spirit of lying as well as the spirit of manipulation they all seem to run together. In the world and in ministry this is probably the most common spirit used to manipulate people and create low self esteem, loneliness, rejection, and abandonment issues.

You will have to learn two things from gossiping; the first one is be careful who you share your personal business with and the second is learn to handle it and move on. I know it sounds easier than it is but one thing I know about people if they find out that something bothers you they will wear you out with it. This is a spirit that you will have to dig into your spiritual gifts and pull out the spirit of discernment so you do not get caught in the middle of a mess. Gossiping can be dangerous and harmful but nevermind what I say let us see what God says.

> *"The words of a talebearer are as wounds, and they go down into the innermost parts of the belly."*
> *Proverbs 26:22 King James Version (KJV)*

> *"He that goeth about as a talebearer revealeth secrets: therefore meddle not with him that flattereth with his lips."*
> *Proverbs 20:19 King James Version (KJV)*

I will say this be very careful who you talk about and what you do especially when it comes to God's people and His spiritual leaders. His word clearly says in Psalms 105:12-15 King James Version (KJV)

> *"When they were but a few men in number; yea, very few, and strangers in it. When they went from one nation to another, from one kingdom to another people; He suffered no man to do them wrong: yea, he reproved kings for their sakes; Saying, Touch not mine anointed, and do my prophets no harm".*

When we look at this scripture touch not my anointed and do my prophet no harm. This is meant literally and figuratively. God will never allow these spirits to supersede his rightful and upright servant. Nor will He ever let you use your mouth or hands to destroy them in terms of their reputation, and the work that they do in His Kingdom. He will redeem you from the hands of the enemy and he will deliver you from the spirits of the enemy if you will allow Him. I know I have only touched the surface with the enemies of life but I wanted you to get an idea of the most common ones that operate in our lives and in the church.

When we look at the word warfare it is a fight between two opposing forces and I gave you the ammunition to win first then I told you some of the common enemies that we are fighting in our own lives. However before I close this chapter I am going to talk a little about the enemies of the church and of the saints. There are many demonic and opposing spirits out there in the realm of the spirit but the Holy Spirit beats all of them. Nevertheless you need to have an idea of what you are up against as a Christian so when the weapon forms against your life it does not prosper.

WITCHCRAFT

Now let us talk about something that is really never taught in the church or that much in the USA. I am talking about witchcraft it is very real and very commonly used against God's people. How ironic no one really takes the time out to school you on how the devil uses people to accomplish his work. Now I am not talking any longer about the enemies of life but I am truly talking about the enemies of God. These are people who work for Satan and use his ways and principles to attack the Christian. I never knew how much witchcraft was used until I begin to get attacked by the works of the devil through his warlocks, witches, witch doctors, and wizards. Let's look at the definition of each one according to the dictionary.

- Witchcraft is the power of practicing witches, black magic and sorcery.
- A witch and a warlock are people who supposedly have supernatural powers by a compact with the devil or evil spirits.
- A witch doctor is a person who practices a type of primitive medicine involving the use of magic, witchcraft, etc…
- Magic is the use of charms, spells and rituals in seeking or pretending to cause or control events, or govern certain natural or supernatural forces.
- Black Magic is magic with an evil purpose.
- Sorcery is supposedly the use of an evil supernatural spirit over people and their affairs; seemingly magic power, influence or charm.
- Wizard is one skilled in magic, witchcraft or sorcery.

Now in my natural mind I cannot phantom why anyone would like to be employed by the devil. Surely you know the end results of this foolish and crazy choice that you have made. I have learned that just as we the Christians have been saved through going to church with our family members on the other hand the devil worshippers have been taught from their family members as well. Well I am a witness that these powers of darkness are real and can do damage to you, your ministry and your purpose if you are not careful. Do not be foolish I know God is greater than any working of the devil but it does not mean the devil is not on his post awaiting his opportunity to devour you.

You would be surprised if you would look back over your life and see how many curses and acts of witchcraft and black magic has come against you. You were ignorant of the devices of the enemy because you had not educated yourself or armed yourself against the workings of the devil. However I believe you now have enough ammunition to combat the devil in the spirit not the natural. It must be done according to the principles of God which we can find in the Bible. Now just so you know that what I have said is real I will give you as always a few scriptures to unveil what the devil has been doing for years in many people's lives.

> *"And I will cut off the cities of thy land, and throw down all thy strong holds: And I will cut off witchcrafts out of thine hand; and thou shalt have no more soothsayers: Thy graven images also will I cut off, and thy standing images out of the midst of thee; and thou shalt no more worship the work of thine hands*
>
> *Micah 5:11-13 King James Version (KJV).*

> *"Because of the multitude of the whoredoms of the wellfavoured harlot, the mistress of witchcrafts, that selleth nations through her whoredoms, and families through her witchcrafts.*

Behold, I am against thee, saith the Lord of hosts; and I will discover thy skirts upon thy face, and I will shew the nations thy nakedness, and the kingdoms thy shame. And I will cast abominable filth upon thee, and make thee vile, and will set thee as a gazingstock."

Nahum 3:4-6 King James Version (KJV)

"Now the works of the flesh are manifest, which are these; Adultery, fornication, uncleanness, lasciviousness, Idolatry, witchcraft, hatred, variance, emulations, wrath, strife, seditions, heresies, Envyings, murders, drunkenness, revellings, and such like: of the which I tell you before, as I have also told you in time past, that they which do such things shall not inherit the kingdom of God."

Galatians 5:19-21 King James Version (KJV)

As I grew up and matured in God I can now look back and identify the attacks of the enemy and using the power of God and His anointing I can overpower the devil and nullify his schemes and plans. This growth and maturity which perfected my call plus the education, revelation and illumination of who God is in this world and in my life gives me total victory over anything that man or Satan can throw at me.

By Now you should have learned enough of the enemies' tactics to shout out loud.

I GOT THE VICTORY IN JESUS NAME!

Victory

"The sting of death is sin; and the strength of sin is the law. But thanks be to God, which giveth us the victory through our Lord Jesus Christ."
1 Corinthians 15:56-57 King James Version (KJV)

We are at our last chapter of this book which means we have made it to our victory. Keep pressing forward we cannot give up now we are this close to our plan, purpose and destiny in God. Our victory in our lives is predicated on these next few topics that we will talk about. One must understand that victory comes through Jesus Christ at the Cross and then it just continue as we learn the principles, statues and commandments of God and apply them. Certainly there is so much to tell you about Jesus life, death and resurrection that I could not tell it all in this book. So we will touch the key points of His life, His will, your life, and your obedience so that we may walk into this victorious life that the Bible speaks about.

Having a victorious life in this world is dependent on you and your perspective. Well let me tell you what I consider a life of victory; a true relationship with the Lord, which consist of living for Christ, walking in the Spirit, being lead by the Spirit, being empowered by the Spirit and when this life is over being ushered into heaven by the Holy Spirit. That's just a quick synopsis of what I consider having a victorious life. Does that mean that we will not have trouble in this life? Of course not even Jesus suffered and died for our sins; we know that trials and tribulations will come but we have to hold on to our faith, glory in tribulations and stand fast on the word of the Lord which states:

> *"By whom also we have access by faith into this grace wherein we stand, and rejoice in hope of the glory of God. And not only so, but we glory in tribulations also: knowing that tribulation worketh patience; And patience, experience; and experience, hope. And hope maketh not ashamed; because the love of God is shed abroad in our hearts by the Holy Ghost which is given unto us. For when we were yet without strength, in due time Christ died for the ungodly. For scarcely for a righteous man will one die: yet peradventure for a good man some would even dare to die. But God commendeth his love toward us, in that, while we were yet sinners, Christ died for us."*
>
> *Romans 5:2-8 King James Version (KJV)*

How many people do you know would die for you even while you were yet their enemy? In case you have not figured that out yet Jesus did and because He died for you and I, we can accept His Death, Burial and Resurrection and learn of Him.

A VICTORIOUS RELATIONSHIP

"Come unto me, all ye that labour and are heavy laden, and I will give you rest. Take my yoke upon you, and learn of me; for I am meek and lowly in heart: and ye shall find rest unto your souls. For my yoke is easy, and my burden is light."
Matthew 11:28-30 King James Version (KJV)

To me this is an invitation from Jesus Christ to me. Anytime I see the Lord say "Come unto me" I recognize that there is victory in Him no matter what the call may entail. "Come unto me" to me means come and get to know me which I take as an opportunity to have a relationship with the Lord. Who can resist that invitation? Surely not I and I hope you can't either. I would love to be able to talk with my Creator and find out all about Him and myself. Nothing better than going to the source to find out why you were created and what is His plans for your life. See a relationship with Him will get you those answers and much, much more and a victorious relationship with Him will establish you in His kingdom and get you eternal life.

What exactly is a relationship? A relationship is defined as kinship and an emotional attachment between individuals. Kinship is the broad term for all the relationships that people are born into or create later in life that are considered binding in the eyes of society. Now let's look at the word victorious; victorious is defined as evincing moral harmony or a sense of fulfillment; triumphant. So is it fair to say a victorious relationship with Christ is considered to be a triumphant kinship between you and God. Now that alone will give you the victory in life.

Just to give you an idea of a victorious relationship with God let me use myself as an example. Before I received salvation I knew God existed but that was the extent of my relationship with Him. I believed there was a God and He created everything and that was pretty much all I could say. However, after going through life and the situations and circumstances that I had to face God became more to me than just a thought or a story. Once I received salvation He became my Savior and as life went on and I begin to get a true revelation of who God was He became my Father. Then when I begin to understand the victory at the Cross He became my Deliverer. Then when I became sick unto death He became my healer (Jehovah Rapha) and a miracle worker. Then once I became a part of the fivefold ministry and some folks begin to lie and persecute me, He became my Redeemer and my banner (Jehovah Nissi). Now as I continue to walk into the calling on my life He has become my teacher and through it all He was my Lord and Master (Adonai).

Truly I could go on and on but it would become boring to you but it is a reality to me. That's why when I look back into the Bible and Moses asked God who shall I say sent me as he was going to confront Pharaoh and deliver God's people from slavery and bondage. I love the answer God gave Moses to tell them: He said tell them "I AM" sent you. Meaning I am what and whoever you need me to be.

> *"And Moses said unto God, Who am I, that I should go unto Pharaoh, and that I should bring forth the children of Israel out of Egypt? And he said, Certainly I will be with thee; and this shall be a token unto thee, that I have sent thee: When*

thou hast brought forth the people out of Egypt, ye shall serve God upon this mountain. And Moses said unto God, Behold, when I come unto the children of Israel, and shall say unto them, The God of your fathers hath sent me unto you; and they shall say to me, What is his name? what shall I say unto them? And God said unto Moses, I Am That I Am: and he said, Thus shalt thou say unto the children of Israel, I Am hath sent me unto you."

Exodus 3:11-14 King James Version (KJV)

See this is one of the many reasons you need to have a personal relationship with God just as Moses did because you need instructions in this road called life. *You need to be able to be honest with yourself and tell God just as Moses did.* When the Lord tells you what your purpose is you will give Him the same thing Moses did which is excuses why you cannot do what God created you to do. When it is time for you to walk into your purpose and destiny there is no place better to get instructions, directions, and reassurance from than your Father Himself. One thing we know about God, He is not a man that He should lie; nor the Son of man that He shall repent; if He said it surely He will do it; and it shall come to pass. This also helps you in your times of insecurities and during your seasons of doubt. Make no mistake people will make you wonder if you were called or chosen by God especially when you are going through hard times because the world's lack of knowledge makes people believe that if you are a true saint you should not have any trouble. How wrong is that thinking? In actuality we have it worse than the non-believer because if you are not born-again Satan already has you. Now this is a Selah moment…..

I want you to think about what I just said and ponder on this scripture:

"He was in the world, and the world was made by him, and the world knew him not. He came unto his own, and his own received him not. But as many as received him, to them gave he power to become the sons of God, even to them that believe on his name."

John 1:10-12 King James Version (KJV).

You must realize that in order for you to become a son or daughter of God you have to believe on Him and His name. This is the start for you developing a relationship with Him. Once you receive power to become an heir (sons of God) truly you have walked into your victorious relationship with God and on or after that everything else from the Lord shall follow. I do not usually quote such a long scripture but I want you to understand when you have a relationship with God you do not have to seek all the other things of life; He will add them to you and if you seek those other things of life and not Him there is also a repercussion.

"And he said, This will I do: I will pull down my barns, and build greater; and there will I bestow all my fruits and my goods. And I will say to my soul, Soul, thou hast much goods laid up for many years; take thine ease, eat, drink, and be merry. But God said unto him, Thou fool, this night thy soul shall be required of thee: then whose shall those things be,

which thou hast provided? So is he that layeth up treasure for himself, and is not rich toward God. And he said unto his disciples, Therefore I say unto you, Take no thought for your life, what ye shall eat; neither for the body, what ye shall put on. The life is more than meat, and the body is more than raiment. Consider the ravens: for they neither sow nor reap; which neither have storehouse nor barn; and God feedeth them: how much more are ye better than the fowls? And which of you with taking thought can add to his stature one cubit? If ye then be not able to do that thing which is least, why take ye thought for the rest? Consider the lilies how they grow: they toil not, they spin not; and yet I say unto you, that Solomon in all his glory was not arrayed like one of these. If then God so clothe the grass, which is to day in the field, and to morrow is cast into the oven; how much more will he clothe you, O ye of little faith? And seek not ye what ye shall eat, or what ye shall drink, neither be ye of doubtful mind. For all these things do the nations of the world seek after: and your Father knoweth that ye have need of these things. But rather seek ye the kingdom of God; and all these things shall be added unto you. Fear not, little flock; for it is your Father's good pleasure to give you the kingdom. Sell that ye have, and give alms; provide yourselves bags which wax not old, a treasure in the heavens that faileth not, where no thief approacheth, neither moth corrupteth. For where your treasure is, there will your heart be also."

Luke 12:18-34 King James Version (KJV).

Now after reading this I think it is self explanatory from both sides of the fence. If you have a relationship with God your outcome will be victorious here on earth and also in heaven but if not; oh well you know the result. One thing a victorious relationship with God is highly dependent on is your prayer life.

A LIFE OF PRAYER

"But we will give ourselves continually to prayer, and to the ministry of the word."

Acts 6:4 King James Version (KJV)

Now when you talk about having a relationship with God I myself consider prayer to be a main part of it. Why? Because according to the Bible, the dictionary and the Bible dictionary prayer is defined as a communication with God. That is the broad definition of prayer. Of course we can get a lot more detailed but let's roll with the broad definition so everyone will comprehend it. It is not that God needs prayer it is simply we need prayer. God is all-knowing (omniscience), all-powerful (omnipotent) and everywhere at the same time (omnipresent). So there is never a moment in life or in this world where God does not know what is going on. The reason why we give ourselves continually to prayer is for spiritual understanding of self, self-advancement in the Kingdom, for a deeper relationship with God and last but not least for a deeper revelation of God. When we prayer all of these things are revealed and unveiled to us even when you are not expecting them.

Prayer is the door to finding out both God's ways and God's thoughts.

See communication with God is not a one way ticket it works two ways. You ask for something and while God is answering you

He reveals something to you about Himself, yourself or the situation you are praying for. What is amazing to me is God's ways are not our ways and His thoughts are higher than our thoughts and prayer is the door to finding out both God's ways and God's thoughts.

> *"For my thoughts are not your thoughts, neither are your ways my ways, saith the LORD. For as the heavens are higher than the earth, so are my ways higher than your ways, and my thoughts than your thoughts. For as the rain cometh down, and the snow from heaven, and returneth not thither, but watereth the earth, and maketh it bring forth and bud, that it may give seed to the sower, and bread to the eater: So shall my word be that goeth forth out of my mouth: it shall not return unto me void, but it shall accomplish that which I please, and it shall prosper in the thing whereto I sent it.*
> *Isaiah 55:8-11 King James Version (KJV)"*

Any time you communicate with someone you should be doing a few things. One is you should be getting to know them and the second is you should be getting an understanding of how they think and also in what manner do they speak. Now here is the good thing about having a relationship with God you have the privilege of the Bible which tells us how he thinks, who He is and what manner He speaks in. It also tells you a very key and important thing not only does he answer pray but whatever word He speaks it shall not return unto Him void but it shall accomplish that which He please, and it shall prosper in the thing where he sends it. This simply means that whatever God speaks to you in prayer whether it be through the still small voice, His word the Bible, dreams, visions, or through a prophecy it will come to pass. Remember we are still talking about prayer and communicating with God those are just God's ways of communicating and answering you back. We also look at prayer as asking God for something and while kneeling down which is according to our traditional mindset but nobody really tells you that God speaks back in many different ways and if you are the only one talking then that's not prayer that's a monolog. Trust me stay around a little longer and silence yourself after your petition and see what God has to say to you, through you and you will find that in prayer He will bless you.

There are many different types of prayers. Just to name a few, there is a prayer of thanksgiving, of adoration, a petitioning prayer, a prayer of worship, a prayer of confession, effective prayer and the most common of them all is the prayer of faith. This is what I call your basic personal prayer line then there is what I call advanced prayers like intercession, travailing and prevailing, binding and loosing, praying in tongues and prayer of healing and deliverance. These prayers take a little more of knowledge, wisdom and understanding of God and His power in the earth realm, the heavenly realm and the atmosphere. There is an old saying although it may not be biblical it is true; "A little prayer, a little power and much prayer much power." I challenge you to increase your prayer and watch God increase your power....

A LIFE OF PRAYER LEADS TO A LIFE OF POWER

> *"But ye shall receive power, after that the Holy Ghost is come upon you: and ye shall be witnesses unto me both in Jerusalem, and in all Judaea, and in Samaria, and unto the uttermost part of the earth."*
>
> Acts 1:8 King James Version (KJV

In this Christian world receiving the Holy Spirit is not an option it is a necessity. Why? Because this is where your power comes from, the Holy Spirit gives you the power to do the work of the Lord and Jesus name gives you the authority. Using Jesus name in the spirit realm is like operating in the power of attorney in the natural realm. It is imperative that you understand how all of this works so that you can be effective in your ministry and in your natural and spiritual life. As a Christian the difference between us and the world is our faith and our power from on high cause us to witness and be a witness. This is why God told His disciples to tarry until you are endowed with power from on high.

> *"And ye are witnesses of these things. And, behold, I send the promise of my Father upon you: but tarry ye in the city of Jerusalem, until ye be endued with power from on high. And he led them out as far as to Bethany, and he lifted up his hands, and blessed them."*
>
> Luke 24:48-50 King James Version (KJV)

Whenever God says behold that means pay close attention I am getting ready to reveal one of my mysteries to you that a carnal mind will not understand. The problem also with many saints is they do not want to tarry for the promises of the Father so they jump ahead and create a few Ishmael's in their lives instead of following the instructions of God and waiting on Isaac. When it comes to power there is no doubt the greatest power you can receive is truly from on high which means from God. Endued means to furnish, as with some talent, faculty, or quality; equip or clothe. Now if you think about what God was telling them don't move from Jerusalem until I clothe and equip you with some talent or quality which is My power from on high. Wow God is still the same today, yesterday and forever more which means if the disciples had to tarry and be clothed and equipped with His power from on high so do we. Many people are operating with no power or the wrong power and some are operating in the right power with no understanding.

Let us look at the word power which means the authority and the ability. See some of us are operating with authority and no ability. Let me explain this; because you have been baptized in the Holy Spirit that does not give you the ability to do the work of the Lord. See there is another part to power that is different from the Holy Spirit being in you, it is called the anointing. The spirit that lives in you is to help you and your spiritual growth but the spirit that is upon you is for us to help others. Let's look at two scriptures that will back up what I am saying so you will not be confused about the power of God. The first one:

> *"And when the day of Pentecost was fully come, they were all with one accord in one place. And suddenly there came a sound from heaven as of a rushing mighty wind, and it filled*

all the house where they were sitting. And there appeared unto them cloven tongues like as of fire, and it sat upon each of them. And they were all filled with the Holy Ghost, and began to speak with other tongues, as the Spirit gave them utterance."

Acts 2:1-4 King James Version (KJV)

Now let us look at the process of what God said and how it works. First you must recognize that your personal Pentecost time has fully come. In other words you have fully surrendered and received salvation and you're ready for your power from on high. Next you must be on one accord with the people around you or if you are alone then you must be on one accord with the Father, the Son and the Holy Spirit. Next step is you will hear a sound from heaven with your spiritual ears that will be heightened to the maximum until it fills the room where you are and then your spiritual eyes will be opened to the heavens. Now here goes the process of God's power and I quote "and it sat upon each of them. And they were all filled with the Holy Ghost, "Notice it was on them and in them before they could operate in the spiritual gift. And they "began to speak with other tongues, as the Spirit gave them utterance." See many did not understand to operate in the anointing of God you need both, you need the power that is in you and you need the power to come upon you. Without the power up on you; you will not be effective when it comes to destroying yokes in the Kingdom of God. Let me give you back up scriptures and you will see it is scriptural based revelation. Whether it is Old Testament or New Testament the spirit must always come upon you for the anointing to exhibit itself.

"And he came to Nazareth, where he had been brought up: and, as his custom was, he went into the synagogue on the sabbath day, and stood up for to read. And there was delivered unto him the book of the prophet Esaias. And when he had opened the book, he found the place where it was written, The Spirit of the Lord is upon me, because he hath anointed me to preach the gospel to the poor; he hath sent me to heal the brokenhearted, to preach deliverance to the captives, and recovering of sight to the blind, to set at liberty them that are bruised, To preach the acceptable year of the Lord. And he closed the book, and he gave it again to the minister, and sat down. And the eyes of all them that were in the synagogue were fastened on him."

Luke 4:16-20 King James Version (KJV)

"The Spirit of the Lord God is upon me; because the Lord hath anointed me to preach good tidings unto the meek; he hath sent me to bind up the brokenhearted, to proclaim liberty to the captives, and the opening of the prison to them that are bound; To proclaim the acceptable year of the Lord, and the day of vengeance of our God; to comfort all that mourn; To appoint unto them that mourn in Zion, to give unto them beauty for ashes, the oil of joy for mourning, the garment of praise for the spirit of heaviness; that they might be called trees of righteousness, the planting of the Lord, that he might be glorified. And they shall build the old wastes, they shall raise up the former desolations, and they shall repair the waste

cities, the desolations of many generations."
Isaiah 61:1-4 King James Version (KJV)

These two scriptures prove that the spirit upon you gives you the anointing you need to do the work of the Lord and to help, deliver and set the captives free. According to the word of the Lord it is the anointing that destroys the yokes. *"And it shall come to pass in that day, that his burden shall be taken away from off thy shoulder, and his yoke from off thy neck, and the yoke shall be destroyed because of the anointing." Isaiah 10:27 King James Version (KJV)* In the midst of talking about the power of God I want to give you some scriptures to build your faith and to give you a revelation of how powerful God's power mixed with faith can be.

SUPERNATURAL POWER-FILLED SCRIPTURES

"And the blood shall be to you for a token upon the houses where ye are: and when I see the blood, I will pass over you, and the plague shall not be upon you to destroy you, when I smite the land of Egypt."
Exodus 12:13 King James Version (KJV)

"He is despised and rejected of men; a man of sorrows, and acquainted with grief: and we hid as it were our faces from him; he was despised, and we esteemed him not. Surely he hath borne our griefs, and carried our sorrows: yet we did esteem him stricken, smitten of God, and afflicted. But he was wounded for our transgressions, he was bruised for our iniquities: the chastisement of our peace was upon him; and

with his stripes we are healed."

Isaiah 53:3-5 King James Version (KJV)

"He sent his word, and healed them, and delivered them from their destructions." Psalm 107:20 King James Version (KJV)
"Verily I say unto you, Among them that are born of women there hath not risen a greater than John the Baptist: notwithstanding he that is least in the kingdom of heaven is greater than he. And from the days of John the Baptist until now the kingdom of heaven suffereth violence, and the violent take it by force."

Matthew 11:11-12 King James Version (KJV)

"But Jesus beheld them, and said unto them, With men this is impossible; but with God all things are possible."

Matthew 19:26 King James Version (KJV)

"Verily, verily, I say unto you, He that believeth on me, the works that I do shall he do also; and greater works than these shall he do; because I go unto my Father. And whatsoever ye shall ask in my name, that will I do, that the Father may be glorified in the Son. If ye shall ask any thing in my name, I will do it."

John 14:12-14 King James Version (KJV)

"And he said unto them, Go ye into all the world, and preach the gospel to every creature. He that believeth and is baptized shall be saved; but he that believeth not shall be damned. And

these signs shall follow them that believe; In my name shall they cast out devils; they shall speak with new tongues; They shall take up serpents; and if they drink any deadly thing, it shall not hurt them; they shall lay hands on the sick, and they shall recover."

Mark 16:15-18 King James Version (KJV)

"So then after the Lord had spoken unto them, he was received up into heaven, and sat on the right hand of God. And they went forth, and preached every where, the Lord working with them, and confirming the word with signs following. Amen."

Mark 16:19-20 King James Version (KJV)

"And Jesus said unto them, Because of your unbelief: for verily I say unto you, If ye have faith as a grain of mustard seed, ye shall say unto this mountain, Remove hence to yonder place; and it shall remove; and nothing shall be impossible unto you."

Matthew 17:20 King James Version (KJV)

Notice the last scripture talks about what you say has power. The power of the tongue is our next victorious topic to learn about.

THE POWER OF THE TONGUE

"Death and life are in the power of the tongue: and they that love it shall eat the fruit thereof."

Proverbs 18:21 King James Version (KJV)

As I was walking into my calling and learning about the power of God I came across something that I had no idea was so powerful, words. I of course learned that God's words were all powerful because He had spoken the world into existence but one thing I was not aware of was that the words that I spoke had power. Many of us walk around speaking carelessly and not recognizing that you are killing yourself with your own words. I learned that I could speak life or death to any given situation that I find myself in. Now once I found out about this I began to change my speaking and my thinking. I had to begin to speak what God's word said and not what the world said. I began to speak what I believe God for no matter what it looks like right now. I began to speak change into my life and keep everything positive and not speak negatively over any situation. Of course it took a lot of time before I began to catch on to what God was trying to get me to do in my life with the power of my tongue and the power of His words I realize nothing would be impossible.

So I began to first renew my mind like Romans 12:2 *"And be not conformed to this world: but be ye transformed by the renewing of your mind, that ye may prove what is that good, and acceptable, and perfect, will of God."* When it comes to the power of the tongue the perfect will of God is to speak life into everything you come in contact with except sin. Not only to speak good things but also speak the truth and think on those things which are true.

"Finally, brethren, whatsoever things are true, whatsoever things are honest, whatsoever things are just, whatsoever things are pure, whatsoever things are lovely, whatsoever

things are of good report; if there be any virtue, and if there be any praise, think on these things. Those things, which ye have both learned, and received, and heard, and seen in me, do: and the God of peace shall be with you."

Philippians 4:8-9 King James Version (KJV)

Actually what you think about is what you will speak about. Jesus said all the things that you have received, heard, seen, and learned in me, do. Look what happens when you do and speak what you have received from the Lord, the God of peace shall be with you. That's one of the benefits of the power of the tongue the others of course would be the rest of the fruit of the spirit. *"But the fruit of the Spirit is love, joy, peace, longsuffering, gentleness, goodness, faith, Meekness, temperance: against such there is no law." Galatians 5:22-23 King James Version (KJV).* When you can comprehend that if you attach the words that you speak to life or death you can speak victory. You can speak true change into your life and when you add the anointing to it, my Lord; you can speak change into the atmosphere. Never let anyone tell you "sticks and stones may break my bones but words will never harm me" that is a lie from the pit of hell. Words can kill you just look back at the world and its people, most of the people who have low self esteem is because of bad words spoken over their lives by someone. Make no mistakes words hurt. To help you get the victory over the future words that may come your way let's talk about putting on the armor of God. For truly bad words spoken into your life is definitely one of Satan's most powerful weapons.

No weapon that is formed against thee shall prosper; and every tongue that shall rise against thee in judgment thou shalt condemn. This is the heritage of the servants of the Lord, and their righteousness is of me, saith the Lord.

Isaiah 54:17 King James Version (KJV)

THE ARMOR OF GOD

"Finally, my brethren, be strong in the Lord, and in the power of his might. Put on the whole armour of God, that ye may be able to stand against the wiles of the devil."

Ephesians 6:10-11 King James Version (KJV)

Finally, my brothers and sisters we all must learn to be strong not in ourselves but in the Lord and in the power of his might. We have talked about the power from on high plus the power of the tongue; now let's talk about the power of putting on God's whole armor. In Ephesians chapter 6 there are some final instructions from the Lord that will keep you protected from the wiles of the devil. The first thing that God lets us know is that we must put on the whole armor not a piece but everything that is considered His armor and we will deal with it as we go along. What is the purpose of the armor? The purpose of putting on the whole armor is so that we may be able to stand against the wiles of the devil. Now what does stand mean and what are the wiles of the devil? Well to *stand* means to remain firm or steadfast, as in a cause; to endure or undergo without harm or damage or without giving way. Now what is *wiles* defined as a trick, artifice, or

> We do not wrestle against flesh and blood but against principalities and powers.

stratagem meant to fool, trap, or entice; deceitful cunning; trickery to lure, beguile, or entice someone.

Now when you put those two words together God is simply telling you to be strong in His power so that you will be able to remain steadfast, firm and be able to remain unharmed when you come against the devils trickery, deceitful traps and enticing strategies. One of the greatest things you can ever learn for a victorious life is we do not wrestle against flesh and blood.

> *"For we wrestle not against flesh and blood, but against principalities, against powers, against the rulers of the darkness of this world, against spiritual wickedness in high places. Wherefore take unto you the whole armour of God, that ye may be able to withstand in the evil day, and having done all, to stand."*
>
> *Ephesians 6:12-14 King James Version (KJV.*

That would be the biggest mistake you could ever make trying to beat the devil with your flesh. Why? Because the devil is a spiritual being using naturally people to do his work. The person is really a front it is the devil that is behind the plan that you are up against. The principalities, powers, rulers of the darkness of this world and spiritual wickedness in high places are who you are fighting so tell me what can your fist or a knife, gun or any other natural weapon do with these demonic spirits.

See if you going to stand in these evil days you must put on the whole armor after having done all to stand. Let's look at the whole armor of God and its purpose and covering.

> *"Stand therefore, having your loins girt about with truth, and having on the breastplate of righteousness; And your feet shod with the preparation of the gospel of peace; Above all, taking the shield of faith, wherewith ye shall be able to quench all the fiery darts of the wicked. And take the helmet of salvation, and the sword of the Spirit, which is the word of God: Praying always with all prayer and supplication in the Spirit, and watching thereunto with all perseverance and supplication for all saints."*
>
> *Ephesians 6:14-18 King James Version (KJV)*

Now here is how God gave it to me to explain to the readers. We know that Paul use the prison guards uniform to explain the pieces of God's armor and what they were protecting. However, God's revelation to me went as such. Speaking and living the truth will gird up your loins. This means back in the old days to gird up your loins meant to get ready for work or battle. So before you go into battle make sure you take the truth with you who is Jesus.

> *"Jesus saith unto him, I am the way, the truth, and the life: no man cometh unto the Father, but by me."*
>
> *John 14:6 King James Version (KJV)*

Now righteousness is your breastplate. Righteousness will cover your heart and keep you on the right path. For without a clean heart your sins are ever before you and your spirit will not be right.

> *"Hide thy face from my sins, and blot out all mine iniquities. Create in me a clean heart, O God; and renew a right spirit within me. Cast me not away from thy presence; and take not thy holy spirit from me."*
>
> Psalm 51:9-11 King James Version (KJV)

Now your feet as it takes the Gospel out will be bringing peace to everyone and everywhere you go. It not only will bring peace but to shod means to cover so you yourself will also be covered with the peace of God which surpass all understanding. However look how God connects the feet with peace.

> *"And if the house be worthy, let your peace come upon it: but if it be not worthy, let your peace return to you. And whosoever shall not receive you, nor hear your words, when ye depart out of that house or city, shake off the dust of your feet. Verily I say unto you, It shall be more tolerable for the land of Sodom and Gomorrha in the day of judgment, than for that city."*
>
> Matthew 10:13-15 King James Version (KJV)

Now next the Lord tells you to take the shield of faith which in reality means your faith is your shield so if you have little faith don't be discourage. It only takes the faith the size of a mustard seed to create a miracle. Faith will put out, extinguish, subdue and destroy those fiery darts that comes to try you or over take you. Don't think it as strange to be tested by the devil and his cohorts but glory that your faith in Christ has protected you.

"If any man speak, let him speak as the oracles of God; if any man minister, let him do it as of the ability which God giveth: that God in all things may be glorified through Jesus Christ, to whom be praise and dominion for ever and ever. Amen. Beloved, think it not strange concerning the fiery trial which is to try you, as though some strange thing happened unto you: But rejoice, inasmuch as ye are partakers of Christ's sufferings; that, when his glory shall be revealed, ye may be glad also with exceeding joy. If ye be reproached for the name of Christ, happy are ye; for the spirit of glory and of God resteth upon you: on their part he is evil spoken of, but on your part he is glorified."
1 Peter 4:11-14 King James Version (KJV)

Now the helmet of salvation will protect your head which consist of your mind. Salvation is like a helmet to the Christian it is a covering. Now you can take that a few different ways. I speak it as our salvation comes through Jesus Christ which is the Head and the covering of the Body of Christ. Many have rejected Him and have no covering of salvation. "This is the stone which was set at nought of you builders, which is become the head of the corner. Neither is there salvation in any other: for there is none other name under heaven given among men, whereby we must be saved. Now when they saw the boldness of Peter and John, and perceived that they were unlearned and ignorant men, they marvelled; and they took knowledge of them, that they had been with Jesus.
Acts 4:11-13 King James Version (KJV)

Now we all know the sword of the spirit which is the word of God will cut through everything in its way.

> *"For the word of God is quick, and powerful, and sharper than any twoedged sword, piercing even to the dividing asunder of soul and spirit, and of the joints and marrow, and is a discerner of the thoughts and intents of the heart. Neither is there any creature that is not manifest in his sight: but all things are naked and opened unto the eyes of him with whom we have to do. Seeing then that we have a great high priest, that is passed into the heavens, Jesus the Son of God, let us hold fast our profession."*
>
> *Hebrews 4:12-14 King James Version (KJV)*

"Praying always with all prayer and supplication in the Spirit" now catch what this verse said praying always with **ALL** prayer and supplications; oops catch this next phrase *"in the Spirit"*. Praying in the spirit not the natural; Satan does not have a clue what you are talking about and neither does his cohorts or people who are trying to destroy you. Praying in the Holy Spirit is a weapon because it builds you up in the faith and separates you from the ungodly.

> *"How that they told you there should be mockers in the last time, who should walk after their own ungodly lusts. These be they who separate themselves, sensual, having not the Spirit. But ye, beloved, building up yourselves on your most holy faith, praying in the Holy Ghost, Keep yourselves in the love*

of God, looking for the mercy of our Lord Jesus Christ unto eternal life."
Jude 1:18-21 King James Version (KJV)

"Watching thereunto with all perseverance and supplication for all saints" my Lord many do not realize you need a watchman in your life and in your ministry. Someone who has the power to watch and pray so that evil and temptation don't over take you.

"For as a snare shall it come on all them that dwell on the face of the whole earth. Watch ye therefore, and pray always, that ye may be accounted worthy to escape all these things that shall come to pass, and to stand before the Son of man."
Luke 21:35-36 King James Version (KJV).

We cannot be like the disciples who fell asleep on Jesus but we must keep watch of one another. Falling asleep can be costly.

"And he cometh, and findeth them sleeping, and saith unto Peter, Simon, sleepest thou? couldest not thou watch one hour? Watch ye and pray, lest ye enter into temptation. The spirit truly is ready, but the flesh is weak. And again he went away, and prayed, and spake the same words."
Mark 14:37-39 King James Version (KJV)

I believe the Holy Spirit has given you a good revelation of the whole armor of God and a few verses mixed in there to enlighten your understanding.

Now let us finish up where we left off

"And for me, that utterance may be given unto me, that I may open my mouth boldly, to make known the mystery of the gospel, For which I am an ambassador in bonds: that therein I may speak boldly, as I ought to speak. But that ye also may know my affairs, and how I do, Tychicus, a beloved brother and faithful minister in the Lord, shall make known to you all things."
Ephesians 6:19-21 King James Version (KJV)

Now the last thing that we can ask for is that utterance be given to us and that we can open our mouth and speak boldly the mysteries of the Gospel which will be given to us by the Holy Spirit. Now when you look up the word *utterance* it speaks about the manner and the power in which you speak. Simply meaning I do not just want to speak with boldness but I need to speak the Gospel with power and according to the word, nature and character of God. Now that is the whole armor of God and truly when you put it on you will walk in VICTORY……

EQUIPPED AND READY TO WALK IN VICTORY

Well well well we have come to the end of our journey and truly it has been a strategic warfare but we have the victory. The method to the madness was if God equipped you with the enemies of life and the enemies of the church He would truly be unveiling and uncovering Satan's strategy for your life. This in return would be opening the door to the strategies of living a victorious life through Christ. While on this journey which I called this road called "life" many of God's and Satan's strategies were given and exposed. However it is up to you whether you want to learn from this and change your life or be defeated by the devil and all his tricks and schemes. My job as the writer was to enlighten you about the everyday life stuff that keeps us bound and in prison and then to equip you with the necessary weapons you needed to defeat your enemy. Well I have done just that!!!!

Now I encourage you to use this book as a tool to help you overcome your personal idiosyncrasies, increase your faith; open up your eyes of understanding about warfare, and to build you up spiritually. So that you can operate in the new spiritual realms and dimensions God has called you to. So I have strategically walked you through the warfare of life and now you have been equipped to live in VICTORY…

> *"And I saw another sign in heaven, great and marvellous, seven angels having the seven last plagues; for in them is filled up the wrath of God. And I saw as it were a sea of glass mingled with fire: and them that had gotten the **victory** over the beast, and over his image, and over his mark, and over the number of his name, stand on the sea of glass, having the harps of God. And they sing the song of Moses the servant of God, and the song of the Lamb, saying, Great and marvellous are thy works, Lord God Almighty; just and true are thy ways, thou King of saints.*
> *Revelation 15:1-3 King James Version (KJV)*

SHALOM!!!
THE END

About The Author

Dr. Karen Deadwyler's Ministry

Dr. Karen Deadwyler is the Visionary of Dr. Karen Deadwyler International and Willing Women of Worship Fellowship and Executive Pastor of Glory Temple Ministries located in North Massapequa, New York. She is married to her best friend Apostle Ronnie Deadwyler for 25 years and counting. Among other things Dr. Karen is an Apostle, Inspirational Empowerment Speaker, Mentor and Life Coach, Preacher, Health Awareness Speaker (Nurse), Columnist and Author of two self-published books.

She is also the Co-founder of a school for the fivefold ministry started in September 2009 in which Apostle Karen is the Director of Education. It is called "God's Training Camp for the Fivefold Ministry" and the first class graduated in June 2010. Dr Karen has a Life Coach Mentoring Program entitled "Will Thou Be Made Whole" established in September 2012. Dr. Karen Deadwyler has been honored with a Citation by Nassau County Legislature for her work in the community and her writing achievements. She has also been recognized and inducted in the 2010 Edition of the Biltmore Who's Who of Executives and Professionals for her work in Christian literature, and dedication to the ministry.

Among her many achievements she has become an Author of two self-published books. *His Miraculous Way* is the first one to be birth out in January 2008 and now book two being birth out January 2010 called *Five Rights Medication For Your Soul*. Dr. Karen is a Licensed Practical Nurse with 28 years of experience in all aspects of nursing. She also worked as an Associate Editor of "The Gospel News Journal" and writes a weekly column called Life Changing Words for a L.I. newspaper called *The Community Journal*. In the midst of all that God allowed her to do and experience she wrote several prayers and revelations of God's names' Her books and prayers are available for sale on her websites http://drkarendeadwyler.com or http://glorytempleministriesinc.ning.com . She hosted her own radio broadcast for a year "You are Next in Line for a Miracle" every Monday & Wednesday @12noon on The Word Network Radio and Mega Live Radio.

She attended House of Refuge Bible Institute in 2008 & 2009 where she received a Bachelor's Degree of Theology majoring in Christian Education from International Theological Seminary of California and also a certificate for completing the School of the Prophets. Apostle Karen has received an Honorary Doctorate of Theology Degree from Tabernacle Bible College & Seminary for her divine wisdom and work in the Kingdom of God as well as her work as an author. For she believes that good training and teaching is an asset to all ministries and churches for when you look back at the word of God in Hosea 4:6 God said "His people die from lack of knowledge."

Bibliography

Thorndike Barnhart Advanced Dictionary, 2nd ed. Glenview, IL: Scott Foresman, 1974.

Youngblood, Ronald FR., ed., F. F. Bruce and R. K. Harrison, consulting eds. Nelson's New Illustrated Bible Dictionary, Nashville, TN: Thomas Nelson, 1995.

DO YOU BELIEVE IN MIRACLES?

I DO - BECAUSE I AM A WALKING, TALKING MIRACLE WRITING THIS BOOK!
Can we truly believe for the impossible not to only receive a miracle, but to be a vessel that the miraculous flows through?

MIRACLES, SIGNS AND WONDERS... A MUST READ!!!!

Just $14.95!

"His Miraculous Way"

READING THIS BOOK DEVELOPS YOUR CHARACTER!

It also delivers your mind, and destroys the works of the enemy by instructing you to be cautious as you walk into your natural and spiritual destiny.
THIS BOOK IS A MUST READ - ESPECIALLY FOR THE BODY OF CHRIST SO WE CAN STOP GOING IN THE WRONG DIRECTION!

Just $18.00!

"Five Rights Medications For Your Soul"

DR KAREN DEADWYLER

An Inspirational & Empowerment Speaker, Health Awareness Speaker (Nurse), Teacher, Writer, Columnist, and Author.

To reach Dr. Deadwyler for Book Signing or to purchase her books - see below!

Phone: (516) 884-0094
Twitter: DrKayD
Facebook: Karen Deadwyler

<http://glorytempleministriesinc.ning.com/profile/KarenDeadwyler>

http://drkarendeadwyler.com